IMPERIAL SPAIN

THE RISE OF THE EMPIRE AND THE DAWN OF MODERN SEA-POWER

BY

EDWARD DWIGHT SALMON

ASSISTANT PROFESSOR OF HISTORY
AMHERST COLLEGE

GREENWOOD PRESS, PUBLISHERS
WESTPORT, CONNECTICUT

PREFACE

The college teacher of general European history is always confronted with the task of finding adequate reading for his classes which is neither too specialized and technical nor too elementary. For many topics, including several of the greatest importance, no such material is at the moment available. Moreover, in too many instances, good reading which undeniably does exist is in the form of a chapter in a larger work and is therefore too expensive for adoption as required reading under normal conditions.

The Berkshire Studies in European History have been planned to meet this situation. The topics selected for treatment are those on which there is no easily accessible reading of appropriate length adequate for the needs of a course in general European history. The authors, all experienced teachers, are in nearly every instance actively engaged in the class room and intimately acquainted with its problems. They will avoid a merely elementary presentation of facts, giving instead an interpretive discussion suited to the more mature point of view of college students.

No pretense is made, of course, that these *Studies* are contributions to historical literature in the scholarly sense. Each author, nevertheless, is sufficiently a specialist in the period of which he writes to be familiar with the sources and to have used the latest scholarly contributions to his subject. In order that those who desire to read further on any topic may have some guidance short bibliographies of works in western European languages are given, with particular attention to books of recent date.

Each *Study* is designed as a week's reading. The division into three approximately equal chapters, many of them self-contained and each suitable for one day's assignment, should make the series as a whole easily adaptable to the present needs of college classes. The editors have attempted at every point to maintain and emphasize this fundamental flexibility.

Maps and diagrams will occasionally be furnished with the text when specially needed but a good historical atlas, such as that of Shepherd, is presupposed throughout.

R. A. N.
L. B. P.
S. R. P.

CONTENTS

vii

IMPERIAL SPAIN

CHAPTER I

FOUNDATIONS OF THE SPANISH EMPIRE

THE mighty empire of 16th-century Spain, which paved the way for the development of European activities in the western hemisphere and upon the western ocean, received its great impetus during the reign of the Catholic Kings, Ferdinand and Isabella. From the voyage they sponsored came the landfall of Columbus, and, in logical sequence, expeditions of discovery and of conquest which destroyed the old limitations of geographical knowledge and began the vast expansion of Europeans over the surface of the globe. From that expansion by men of West Europe into the New World and the Far East came far-reaching consequences. First there came the transplanting of western civilization, the establishment of outposts in those distant regions, and the extension of old states into enormously enlarged empires. There followed a sweeping alteration in the life and thoughts of the European peoples through new economic opportunities and the more important opening of new horizons, mentally as well as terrestrially. It was because the men of the Iberian peninsula led in the combined activities of exploration and of empire-building, and because the other maritime nations of Europe attained their naval and colonial development from bitter struggles against the menace of the dominant Spanish Empire, that we can

3

profitably examine the growth of that widespread imperial structure and the effects of its contacts with its national rivals.

To understand the story of Spain's imperial expansion it is necessary to have in mind the background of her development. Thrust out as a westward and southerly outpost of the European continent, the peninsula known to the Romans as Iberia served as the boundary of the Mediterranean Sea, with its southernmost tip at the Straits of Gibraltar, one of the fabled Pillars of Hercules. That hero, in setting up his pillars, was marking the western limits of the world of classic antiquity, as indicated by their legendary motto *Ne Plus Ultra,* so that the mariner steering toward the setting sun might be warned to proceed no farther. But at the same time that the rugged peninsula formed the western barrier of the ancients, its long Atlantic coastline looked out upon the unknown reaches of that mysterious sea and invited the residents of Iberia to venture into its feared uncertainty. Another geographical feature of no less importance for the history of the peninsula is its nearness to Africa; joined together in comparatively recent geologic times, the two sides of the Straits of Gibraltar are separated by only some eleven miles of water, a slight obstacle to the movements of men back and forth from North Africa to Spain. If the water gateway of the Mediterranean furnished no serious barrier to travel north and south, such a barrier did exist naturally to the north, where the mountain chain of the Pyrenees discouraged intercourse with France and tended to shut the dwellers of Iberia in upon themselves. Thus the peninsula, with water on three sides and with the Bay of Biscay and the Pyrenees on the fourth, northern, side was geographically almost an island. As a direct consequence of this natural situation the development of the Iberian peoples was largely insular, affected by contacts with North Africa, but save for occasional and irregular periods, removed from the influences and currents of activity of the rest of western Europe. Moreover the internal geography has exerted no small influence upon the character of the Iberian people and the course of their history. Topographically the region is marked by an elevated plateau which extends as a rolling plain with an average elevation of around 2,500 feet above sea-level and which consequently brings to the interior clear, dry air and rapid, violent changes in temperature. This plain is broken by several rugged mountain ranges, running in a generally east-west direction, and rising to respectable heights, notably the peak of Mulhacén in the Sierra Nevadas in the extreme south which has an altitude of 11,420 feet. The high mean elevation of the plateau and the cutting off of rain clouds by the mountains result in the interior being semi-arid, with no rain through the middle of the summer and with irrigation a necessity for the growing of vegetables and grain. The rivers have the characteristics of streams in a desert country, alternating between a thin trickle or empty bed in the dry season and a raging torrent during the period of rain. Moreover, they descend so abruptly from the mountains and the high interior plateau that they are full of rapids, are swift, and in general of little use for commerce or intercourse, because of the difficulty of navigating them. An exception must be made for the Guadalquivir, the lower course of which is navigable for ocean-going craft up to Seville, fifty-four miles from the river mouth. But the rivers as a whole and the mountain ranges cause the land surface to be divided into quite sharply defined regions, as a glance at a physical map of the Iberian peninsula will show. Hence from the earliest times its inhabitants have tended toward regionalism and separatism and the development of a local individuality; they have shown a consciousness of the distinctive life and ways of each small area; they have felt loyalty to the locality; and they have marked their differences from the people over the range or across the valley.

EARLY HISTORY

In this land of Iberia evidences of human habitation and activity reach back to ancient times. Not only are there remains of the life of prehistoric men in caves, as at Altamira, where wall-painting and implements show the stage of development of paleolithic men, but records arising from the contacts of people from the outside world with Iberians give us knowledge of the region as early as the 12th century B.C. From an early day the adventurous traders of Phœnicia knew of Spain, whence they carried back to the eastern end of the Mediterranean, wool, some metals, tuna and eels, and especially the sea-snails which furnished the shells for making the famous purple dye of Tyre. Traders and merchants that they were, the Phœnicians set up trading posts, but did not exploit the country. Tradition assigns the date 1130 B.C. to their town of Gadeira, the modern Cadiz, and traces the derivation of the name of Malaga on the Mediterranean coast of Spain to Mel-Karth, the Phœnician equivalent of Hercules. This is the country spoken of in the Old Testament as Tarshish (ca. 990 B.C.) and the Phœnicians reported finding along the southern coasts of Spain a people calling themselves Tartessians, who had come from Africa originally and whose name recalls the Tarshish which sent to Solomon the romantic tribute of ivory, apes, and peacocks. The Tartessians are supposed to have pointed to the merchants of Tyre and Sidon the way to the tin mines of Cornwall, opening the commerce the Phœnicians were carrying on with Britain by the 5th century B.C. The next comers from the East were Greeks who had pushed trading and colonizing activities westward along the northern Mediterranean shore, had founded Massalia, the ancestor of the port of Marseilles, and had begun to trade in eastern Spain in 700 B.C. Like their earliest predecessors farther south, these Greeks contented themselves with establishing posts on the coast and made no attempt to conquer wide territory or to found colonies inland. To Grecian merchants this land was Hesperia, the land of the evening sun, and the settlers in their trading towns through the succeeding generations carried on the Hellenic traditions of civilization. Their religious and political ideas impressed the hardy, warlike natives of the interior, however, leaving some influence, particularly on the religious notions of the primitive people.

These natives as a general stock occupying the greater part of the peninsula appear to have belonged to the Mediterranean grouping of peoples and are generally called Iberians. The problem of their original location and their relationships to other European and African races, forms a highly controversial question; but whether the Iberians came from the north and advanced across Spain into North Africa, or whether they came from the south and occupied Spain from an African center, or whether they were indigenous to Iberia, it is clear that the Iberians were in possession of most of the peninsula at an early date and that they were closely akin in physical characteristics to the Berber peoples of North Africa. Subsequent to the contacts of eastern traders in the south, the Iberians received a wave of Celtic migration from the north. Somewhere around 450 B.C. a branch of the Celts swarmed into the northwestern and northern parts of the peninsula and began to advance among the Iberians. The two peoples got on well together, on the whole, after initial hostility, and while the newcomers remained concentrated in some numbers in the north and northwest, that is in Galicia, the Asturias, and in northern Portugal, where they first halted, others of them spread into the central and eastern regions. Here the older population and the invading Celts fused and intermarried to form a composite people known as Celt-Iberians, who made up the inhabitants of the great central plateau and who are mentioned in the writings of Herodotus. These primitive peoples exhibited strongly marked tendencies toward independence, individuality, and impatience of outside authority; they tended to form small local or village groups (*pueblos*) rather than large tribal organizations and to these *pueblos* they were devotedly attached. Thus the effects of the physiographic nature of the country intensified this tendency and fostered the typical Spanish inclination to gather in towns, to lean toward localism, and to be independent in the extreme.

Another element in the primitive population of the peninsula is the group of people in the north known as the Basques. The controversy over racial origins and relationships likewise rages around this group and with even greater violence than in the case of the Iberians. Linguistically these northerners in Iberia differ from all their neighbors in early times and at present.[1] Although the riddle of the origin of the Basque people and the Basque language may never be conclusively settled, the presence of that hardy and resistant strain of people on both slopes of the western Pyrenees has contributed to the development of Spaniard and Frenchman alike.

Next in point of time to the Greeks the primitive inhabitants of Spain came into contact with outsiders from the older areas of civilization in the East in the persons of the Carthaginians. Carthage had been founded by Phœnician traders around 800 B.C., had become a flourishing trading empire, and when in 585 B.C. the attacks of Nebuchadnezzar of Chaldea had broken up the Phœnician state, the daughter colony became the refuge for many of the fugitives from Tyre and Sidon. Others of the Phœnicians fled to their cities in southern Spain and began close relations with their kinsmen in Carthage. Difficulties with their Iberian neighbors led these Phœnicians to appeal to the

---

[1] Instead of an inflective language which modifies the root of a word to mark changes in case or tense, the Basque is agglutinative, that is, it adds syllables to indicate changes in noun and verb, like such primitive tongues as Eskimo and North American Indian. Hence the verb includes in one word all the pronouns, adverbs, and other parts of speech. For example, there are fifty possible forms of the third person singular, present indicative of the verb *to give*. The language lacks generalized ideas so that there is no word for *brother* and one must say *brother of the man* or *brother of the woman*. The old proverb that the devil studied Basque seven years and learned two words can be appreciated by the following sample of a Basque word, "Azpicuelagaraycosaroyarenberecolarrea" which means "the lower field of the high hill of Azpicuela." On the basis of language, philologists have proved the Basque people to be relics of almost every fabled lost people or distant race, including the inhabitants of Atlantis, the Etruscans, the Picts, the Egyptians, and various kinds of Asiatics and American Indians.

Carthaginians for aid. The latter sent an expedition which defeated the natives in 516 and which served to acquaint the Carthaginians with the desirability of the country so that they turned against the Phœnicians who had invited them and conquered the coast towns, holding them for their own and getting possession of the commerce of the southern part of the peninsula. The Carthaginians then carried the war into the interior, took Cadiz, fought the Massalian Greeks at Ampurias, a great commercial post on the east coast in modern Catalonia, and by about 500 B.C. the new conquerors were firmly established from Cadiz to Cartagena. For two centuries and a half Carthaginian domination prevailed over southern and eastern Iberia. The conquered region became a part of Carthage's great colonial empire around the south shores of the Mediterranean and the mercantilist policy of the conquerors kept Spain as a source of revenue and trade for the imperial city. The mineral wealth from Iberia went to adorn Carthage and the commerce of the peninsula remained a strict Carthaginian monopoly from which alien traders were rigidly excluded.

Meanwhile a dangerous rival had been growing on the northern edge of the Mediterranean, and Rome in her youthful vigor was challenging the older imperial establishment of Carthage. Such middle points in the Mediterranean periphery as Sicily and Spain were bound to be zones of conflict and the verdict of the two Punic wars was to transfer both Sicily and Spain to Roman control. Spain had played no inconsiderable part in the struggle. Following the first war Hamilcar Barca had come with some of the discontented veterans from Carthage to the peninsula and had extended Punic sway northward. His son Hannibal had grown to maturity in Spain, had married a Spanish wife, had gained valuable military experience at the head of Carthaginian forces there, and had appreciated the military virtues of the Celt-Iberians to such an extent that when he moved out of Iberia for the famous invasion of Italy in the second Punic war, his army is reputed to have had a quarter of its strength made up of Celt-Iberians. The final stages of this second war were fought on Spanish soil in the campaigns of Scipio Africanus who broke the Carthaginian domination of the peninsula. Scipio's victories over Hasdrubal, the brother of Hannibal and commander in Iberia, culminated in the capture of Cadiz by the Romans in 206 B.C., and with this city fell Carthaginian rule. Before the civilizing and instructive genius of the Romans, now presented with the opportunity to conquer and Romanize the peninsula, the Carthaginian and earlier eastern influences disappeared, leaving only fleeting traces: a trading tradition, some experience of agriculture, of stock-raising, of mining and of galley-building, a few place names, and some shreds of religious notions.

ROMANIZATION

For the next six centuries Rome was to hold Iberia and to make her impress on the land so strongly that spiritual and material evidences of her presence are still discernible today. The new masters of the country found it no easy task to subdue the natives. While the regions to the south and east with their long experience with outsiders and their settled life in commercial cities were ready to accept Roman rule, the ruder, untamed *pueblos* of the interior and of the north resisted and forced Rome to spend two centuries before her conquest was complete. In 38 B.C. an edict of Augustus to regularize the taxation of Iberia bears witness to the success of Romanization. From that time forward the peninsula was to be a loyal and integral part of the Empire and its population valuable contributors to the life of the Roman world. The Iberian provinces gave to Rome such Emperors as Trajan, Hadrian, and Theodosius, and such intellectual figures as the two Senecas, Ovid, Lucan, Martial, and Quintillian. The preceding foreign occupations of the land had strengthened the individualistic tendencies of the Iberian people; Rome saved them from further development of a purely tribal sort by forcing the idea of the state on a society made of separate small groups and separate towns. But Rome could not eradicate the earliest Iberian characteristics of a strong sense of individuality, of intense personal independence, and of tenacious local patriotism.

Under the Empire a real fusion of native and Roman elements took place so that Spain received her civilization direct from Rome. Many Roman colonists went out to Iberia and in the course of time a considerable intermixture of blood resulted. The completeness of Romanization of the unmixed physical stocks of Celt-Iberians as well, made Latin language and ways prevail over pre-existing speech and customs. Save for Basque, the tongues of modern Iberia, Spanish, Portuguese, Catalan, and the dialect variants, are all Romance languages descended from the spoken Latin of Roman soldier and merchant. In the sphere of political organization Rome had precious lessons to teach. She divided the country into provinces and improved it by constructing great systems of roads through its length and breadth. She made a lasting contribution in the organization of cities on a self-governing basis. Here the ancient habit of the natives of gathering around the *pueblo* furnished an incentive which the work of conquest furthered; around the fortified camps and military posts of the legions, towns sprang up, as the names of present cities testify. Modern Leon was the *Urbs Septimis Legionis,* Saragossa. was *Cæsar Augusta,* and Merida was *Emerita Augusta.* By treating with towns during the subjugation the Romans increased the prestige of those units and by granting wide privileges of local autonomy to those towns which submitted without resistance, the Romans laid the foundation for a tradition of municipal democracy. The question of how much the city governments derive their political complexion from Rome and how much they owe to native origin is controversial but it is clear that the characteristic of democratic control was allowed by the Romans and was paralleled in other provinces. The principle of self-government found institutional expression in the *populus* or assembly of the citizens to pass on matters affecting the city and to appoint officers to run the city's affairs, and in the *curia* or locally selected executive committee to supervise the work of the elected officials. As elsewhere in the Empire Rome brought her great system of law and the worship of her gods and later of the Emperor. With the recognition of Christianity the new faith spread rapidly through Spain where the population accepted it with zeal. Church councils became important in the church and in the general life of the peninsula, supplanting the provincial gatherings of the imperial organization which had been political consultations combined with the formal discharge of the duties of Emperor-worship. Such a church council at Toledo in 400 A.D. fixed the Romanized Celt-Iberians as fanatically orthodox Christians, although the religious intensity of the people of the country had been manifested previously by the formation of numerous heresies by Spaniards, notably the Priscillian.

THE VISIGOTHS

Like other parts of the Empire, Iberia experienced the weakening of the Roman system and the incursion of migrating groups of the Germanic barbarians in the 5th century. In 409 the Vandals, Suevi, and Alani entered the peninsula from southern Gaul with but slight hindrance from the feeble Roman garrisons. Five years later the Visigoths, who had spread through Gaul after their capture of Rome, crossed the Pyrenees and defeated their kindred tribesmen who had preceded them in Iberia. The Vandals in 429 passed across the Straits of Gibraltar to overrun North Africa and set up a kingdom there, while the Visigoths replaced them as the dominant power in the peninsula. From 466, when these Germanic warriors threw off the last pretense of obedience to Rome and of alliance with the Emperor, until they in turn fell before the military might of the Moslems, the Visigoths ruled Iberia. Originally holding a great territory on both sides of the Pyrenees with their headquarters on the Rhone and later at Toulouse, the Visigoths were beaten south of the mountain barrier by Clovis and his newly Christianized Franks in 507. From that time on, their capital was at Toledo, in the heart of Spain, and save for a strip of land along the Mediterranean in southern France, the Visigothic kingdom was established in the

Iberian land. The Visigothic sway was the dominance of a military minority; the Romanized population outnumbered the Germanic newcomers by about five to one. That disparity in numbers combined with the superior organization and cultivation of the Romanized inhabitants to subject the Visigoths to Romanization and absorption into the peoples they ruled. For a time the mingling of barbarian and civilized provincial was retarded by the religious difference between them. The Visigoths were one of the Germanic peoples converted to Arian Christianity and consequently a wide gulf existed between their form of the Christian faith and that of the mass of their subjects who were orthodox Athanasians and inclined to fanatic insistence on orthodoxy. By 587, however, the weak King Reccared succumbed to the pressure of the churchmen and the Athanasian majority and carried the Visigothic nation with him into the orthodox camp. That change of religion marked a turning-point. The forceful and independent tribesmen who had come into the peninsula earlier altered rapidly after 587, imitated the softer ways of the Roman provincials, and declined in strength and toughness. The succeeding monarchs fell under the complete dominance of the bishops as the Visigoths abjured their Arian heresy. These erstwhile upstanding warriors lost their military qualities, lost their Germanic language, and finally lost even their identity and became indistinguishably merged into the Romanized population they had conquered but could not master culturally.

The importance of the Visigothic kingdom however lay, not in its relatively short-lived political existence, but in its service as a carrier of Roman things to later times. The period of the Visigoths in Iberia is one of transition between the era of Rome and the era of the middle ages. The Visigoths were assiduous copiers of the ways and organization they found in the peninsula and although the Roman institutions they imitated had declined from their earlier vigor and effectiveness, the Visigoths preserved much that was Roman for further development in medieval Spain. Outstanding among the Roman survivals through Visigothic activity was law. The Goths showed an extreme fondness for lawbooks; the Visigoths early wrote down their customary Germanic law as a result of observing the advantages of a written over an oral code, and in 506 their king Alaric II had a great codification of the Roman law made for the use of Visigothic judges. The legal concepts of the German barbarians included the personal idea of law, that every man was entitled to be judged by the system of law into which he was born. Consequently the provincial population under Visigothic sway could expect to be judged by the law of the old Empire, and Visigothic judges and rulers must have for their guidance a statement of Roman rules of law. For this purpose the *Breviary of Alaric,* or summary, was drawn from the Theodosian Code and the *Institutes* of Gaius. This was the best of the barbarian codes of Roman law (called the *Lex Romana Barbarorum*), and, because it was such a good version, the Breviary was used widely outside of Iberia. Hence it was the most useful instrument for the transmittal of Roman Law to the Europe of the Dark Ages and, until the rediscovery of Justinian's great code in the later 11th century, Alaric's handbook was in the West a leading source of that system of jurisprudence.

MOSLEMS AND THE RECONQUEST

Meanwhile the 7th century saw the advancing might of Mohammedanism force its way westward through North Africa against the bitter, stubborn resistance of the Berber population of the former Roman provinces of Mauretania. Uncompromising foes of the Arab hosts of the Prophet, the Berbers finally accepted the faith of Islam from conviction but not from conquest, and became as fanatically earnest Moslems as their remote racial kindred the Celt-Iberians had become Christians. Early in the 8th century these new converts to Islam and their Arab co-religionists took advantage of the weakened state of the Visigothic kingdom to cross the straits into Iberia. After a reconnoitring expedition in 710, a Berber commander named Tarik led an army of 7,000 into Spain in 711 and defeated and killed the Gothic King Roderick at the head of his warriors.[1] This battle, a three-day struggle formerly called the Battle on the Guadalete, destroyed the mobile fighting forces of the kingdom. Although there were many walled cities to be taken and battles still to be fought before the followers of Mohammed could claim mastery of the peninsula, the organization of the Visigoths went to pieces with the slaying of Roderick and the overthrow of his army. In a series of rapid movements the Moslem columns attacked and captured key cities, Malaga, Cordova, Seville, and the Visigothic capital, Toledo, which fell almost without a blow in its defence. Within the ranks of Islam in Spain there was always to be friction and ill-feeling

[1] The modern *Gibraltar* comes from the Arabic *Jebl-ul-Tarik*, meaning "the rock of Tarik" and thus perpetuates the name of the Moslem leader.

between the Berber and Arab elements, each people being different in temperament and each feeling jealousy of the other. An early example of such opposition cropped up during the rapid advance of Tarik's force when the Arab governor of *Ifrikya* (Africa) removed the Berber leader from the command and brought a temporary halt to the conquest northward. In spite of this and other similar interruptions, however, the invaders carried their wave of victory to the Pyrenees in 719 and passed across into southern France, gaining territory along the Mediterranean and reaching a high point at the Battle of Tours in 732. In the rapid spread of Moslem arms in Spain the conquerors encountered no organized opposition since the decadent Visigothic power had completely disintegrated and it was as local groups that the Christian inhabitants offered resistance.

Yet in the face of this sweeping tide of military success there were elements in the country and its people which stood against the invaders. The old independent spirit of the Iberian and the rugged character of the land combined to set in motion a reaction against the Moslems, a reaction destined to achieve the final expulsion of Mohammedan power from the peninsula in the very year of the discovery of America. In the year 718, however, the ultimate decision in the conflict between cross and crescent lay almost eight centuries ahead in the mists of the future; what was important at the moment was the flaming out of Christian resistance in scattered and local centers of opposition to Islam. Traditionally the movement started with a small band of followers of one Pelayo, a warrior who claimed descent from the Gothic Kings. This band of Christians began fighting the victorious invaders in the mountains of the Asturias in the northwest and, according to the legend, their first success was the repulse of an army of the Moslems from the Cave of Covadonga. Here in 718 the Moslems drove Pelayo and his followers to take refuge, but thanks to divine assistance, the Christians drove off their assailants and inflicted so crushing a defeat upon the infidels that as a military engagement it partakes of the miraculous, if the legendary details be taken as anywhere near true. Some 200 years later the Bishop of Salamanca related that at the Cave of Covadonga, Pelayo and his thirty men killed the Moslem general and 124,000 of his men, drove 63,000 more into the river to die by drowning, and forced 375,000 other infidel soldiers to take refuge across the Pyrenees. Other chroniclers of the glorious beginning of the Christian Reconquest of the peninsula outdo themselves in presenting the magnitude of Pelayo's triumph. Even in the 17th century the celebrated Jesuit, Father Mariana, put into his General History of Spain a highly colored version of the Covadonga victory. Although it is impossible to accept the legends at their face value, it is clear that in the highlands of the north and northwest of Iberia, where remnants of all the defiant peoples had taken refuge from conquering majorities since the time of the Celts, fierce resistance to Islam burst forth in guerilla warfare and kept small groups of Christians independent of Moslem domination. It is not surprising that with easy conquests of the rich and populous towns of Southern Gaul awaiting them across the mountains, the Arab-Berber host should have preferred to sweep on rather than to take the time to stamp out the separate sparks of hostility in the ridges and glens of the Pyrenees and Cantabrians.

Following the repulse of the Moors [1] from Covadonga, Pelayo and his followers added territory and were joined by similar groups of Christians until before long their lands became known as the Kingdom of the Asturias, with Pelayo as the monarch. His capital was the village of Canga de Onís, later moved successively to the towns of Oviedo and Leon. By taking advantage of the feuds between Berber and Arab the successor of Pelayo extended the limits of the little kingdom. Uniting temporarily with his Christian neighbors, the Basque tribes of the western Pyrenees, he raided the Moslem territory to the southward. To the west the kingdom expanded through Galicia and northern Lusitania to the Atlantic and to the east it spread along the Biscay coast. By the end of the 8th century the Asturian monarchs controlled practically all the northwest of the peninsula, although the Moorish habit of devastating the lands from which they were driven created a wide belt of uninhabited country between the two forces. Through-

[1] Explanation of a few terms is necessary. The word *Moor* is the general Spanish term for a Mohammedan; in origin it means an inhabitant of the Roman province of Mauretania in North Africa, but the Spanish usage applied it to any Mohammedan, whatever his geographical home. *Islam,* from the Arabic, meaning "safety through submission to the will of God," is a designation for the faith of Mohammed and for its adherents. *Moslem* (in English also spelled in a variety of ways, as *Muslim, Mussulman,* &c.), from the same root and meaning literally "one who has sought safety through submission," is a term for an individual Mohammedan or for the equivalent of the adjective Mohammedan. *El-Andalus,* meaning "the West," was the Arabic name for the conquered land or province of Iberia and from it comes the Spanish name *Andalusia* for the southern portion of the peninsula, where Moorish political control and customs lingered longest. *Emir* is the word for an Arabic prince or governor. *Caliph,* meaning "successor," is the head of the Moslem world, originally in both the political and the religious sense.

out the middle ages the warfare between cross and crescent was to be largely a war of raids and not a war of pitched battles. Consequently the Christians early adopted the practice of building castles on their borders and in newly won regions. In the first beginning of the Christian Reconquest the Church played an important part; the clergy spread the belief that Covadonga represented divine intercession and urged all Christians to join the holy war against the infidel. Therefore when the early zeal began to flag and when kings of the Asturias began to treat with and pay tribute to the Moslem rulers in the south, when the population along the borders began to settle down amicably beside nearby Moslems and when Christians began to show an interest in the learning and luxury of the cultivated Arabs, the Christian priests restored something of the old religious fervor by the aid of another miracle. The miracle was the reputed finding of the body of Saint James the Greater in a remote spot in the Galician mountains, a clear indication that God favored the Christians of that land in their conflict with Islam. This had far-reaching importance. It made a great national legend, it provided the Spaniards with a war-cry, the name Santiago (Saint James), and it changed a guerilla border warfare for physical existence into a Crusade; it laid the foundations of the Spanish monarchy in close conjunction with the Christian faith. Pilgrims flocked to the shrine of Santiago at Compostela in ever-increasing numbers and it became one of the greatest goals of pilgrimage for all of western Europe. A church was built at the site and the international significance of Santiago as well as its general popularity as a shrine is reflected in the

Spanish designation of the Milky Way as "the road to Santiago."

Yet in spite of momentous beginnings for the Moslem conquest of the peninsula on the one hand, and for the Christian reaction (with miraculous assistance as it was currently believed) against the Moorish domination, on the other, both sides suffered periodic vicissitudes and reverses. To the friction between semi-savage Berbers and haughty Arabs was added the general weakening of the power of the Caliphs and the resultant break-up of authority in Moorish Spain among petty chieftains. In 756 a refugee from the defeated dynasty of the Ommayad Caliphs who had escaped from the murder of his house at Damascus, established unified political power in the peninsula. His successors for about 300 years maintained Moorish Spain as a typical oriental despotism and brought it to a high point in civilization. One of these Ommayad rulers, Abd-ar-Rahman III, was sufficiently powerful to proclaim himself in 929 Caliph of the Mohammedan world and to his capital of Cordova, part of Islam looked for the successor of Mohammed. Under Abd-ar-Rahman III, Cordova was the chief center of culture in the West and throughout the 10th century the Spain of the Moslems was the one bright spot intellectually in Europe. In general the Moors displayed remarkable toleration toward other religious faiths and permitted Jews and Christians to live in peace in Moslem cities, practicing their own religions in return for the payment of a regular tribute to the conquerors. The Ommayad line declined in the 11th century and died out in 1031, with the result that the Moorish state again broke into a number of small principalities.

The Christians meanwhile had been retarded in their recovery by internal difficulties. The nobles proved a serious problem for the Christian monarchs. Unlike the kings, the barons were not directly concerned in the success of the Reconquest and they showed the usual feudal fondness for private war, for fighting among themselves, and for resisting the king and his attempts to establish supremacy over them. They were helped in the latter interest by the remains of the old Visigothic tradition of elective kingship; it was only after a struggle that the kings were able to fix the principle that the son of a king should succeed his father as a matter of hereditary right. Strangely enough the monarchs themselves contributed to the weakening of the royal power by the early habit of dividing their kingdom among all their sons. These factors not only lessened the effectiveness of what central government there was, but naturally hampered the conduct of the great Crusade.

LEON-CASTILE

Of similar effect was the deep-seated jealousy between the several Christian states, which prevented frequent coöperation and made combinations against the common enemy both rare and short-lived. In this the old elements of localism and separatism are visible; they were at work in the hostility between nobles and between nobility and crown, and were to result in still further division among the Christians. During the advance in territory the kingdom of the Asturias expanded into the elevated plain of Leon in the 9th century, where it made its center and the name of which it took as the designation of the kingdom. The eastern portion of the recovered land was hard to hold and the

Kings set up there a system of marches, giving extensive authority to counts who were strong enough to defend the region against the Moorish counter-attacks. The name of Castile became fixed to this section because of the need of throwing out castles in that debatable territory.

In the 10th century an ambitious "Count of Burgos" in Castile took the first steps toward securing independence from his overlord the king of Leon, by treachery, intrigue, and open rebellion, even by allying with the Moors against his sovereign. From this activity came autonomy for the County of Castile, then recognition of equality with the kingdoms of Leon and of Navarre. Eventually marriage alliances with the parent kingdom brought the crowns of Leon and of Castile together in 1230 in a permanent union. The name of the newer realm assumed most importance and Castile took the lead in the combined state. Localism triumphed in this evolution, but the war against the infidel lost ground while Counts of Castile were struggling to escape from Leonese control and while Kings of Castile were bickering with Kings of Leon or Navarre. Thus with internal dissension on either side Christian and Moslem were frequently diverted from fighting their religious enemies.

Great weakness in the Moorish ranks called forth more persistent Christian pressure. In the Moslem disunion before the coming of the first Ommayad, Christians had reached to the Douro River, and with the dwindling of the Caliphate of Cordova in 1031 the Crusade pushed to the Tagus River. In 1085 Alfonso VI of Castile and Leon captured the old Gothic capital of Toledo with the support of a true crusading army which included knights from the European world across the Pyrenees. Among those foreign knights were two sons of the ducal house of Burgundy each of whom the victorious Alfonso rewarded with a bride from among his daughters and with a countship in western Leon. One county was the northern part of the Roman province of Lusitania, then called the County of Portugal, and from this grant was to evolve the independent kingdom of Portugal, ruled by the descendants of the Burgundian knight and the daughter of Alfonso VI.

At this juncture it appeared likely that the Moorish power in the peninsula might go to pieces and that the Christian states might drive out the disunited Moslems. The Mohammedan cause was saved by the rise to strength of first one reforming movement and then another, among the Berber Moslems of interior North Africa. The first group of Berber zealots was that of the Almoravides; starting to purify Islam of worldliness and of corruptions which had crept into the faith of the Prophet, these Berbers fought their way to control over their co-religionists in North Africa and spread their Empire across the straits. The Almoravides brought a fresh enthusiasm and a new stock of vigorous warriors to Iberia and drove back the Christians after beating Alfonso VI in a decisive battle in 1086. Toledo remained in Castilian hands however. The Christians were troubled by internal difficulties and Moslem power revived under the reformers who ruled Spain from their center in North Africa. Prosperity was too much for the Almoravides and their strength declined so that they fell easy prey to another religious reforming sect of Berbers, the Almohades, who supplanted them in control of Moorish Spain between 1144 and 1147. From a defeat at the hands of the

Almohades in 1195 the Christians learned a lesson. They rose above jealousy and localism to combine under the leadership of Castile in a united attack on the infidel. The result was a great Christian victory at Las Navas de Tolosa in 1212, the most weighty Christian triumph over the Moslems in the centuries of the Reconquest. The Almohades were broken and although the discordant elements among the victors would not hold together to capitalize the victory, the backbone of Moorish military strength was shattered.

There remained three centers of Moorish power, strong local concentrations, at Valencia, Murcia and Jaen, in the southeast and east of the peninsula. Here the Moslems were firmly established, but to lead the forces of the Reconquest there was the finest figure of the Crusade and one of the ablest rulers of medieval Spain, Saint Ferdinand (Ferdinand III) of Castile. Thanks to his unwavering purpose and military qualities Cordova and Seville fell to the Christians and the Moors were restricted to the Emirate or kingdom of Granada in the extreme south. Ferdinand III could have secured the one remaining Moslem area, but, unlike his predecessors in the line of Christian monarchs, Ferdinand was true to his word. The Emir of Jaen had submitted to Ferdinand and had aided him to capture Seville. For that reason the King of Castile would not attack his vassal but permitted the Emir to withdraw to the region about Granada. The state of Granada remained a dependency of the crown of Castile and in that shrunken remnant of the old Moorish caliphate the Moslem retained a foothold in the south when Saint Ferdinand died prematurely in 1252. In the 14th century the Moors made a last concerted effort to recover the peninsula with the combined forces of Granada and Morocco.   But Alfonso XI of Castile defeated the Moslems at the Rio Salado (1340) in Andalusia, thanks to using a fleet of Iberian and hired Genoese galleys to control the waters between Gibraltar and North Africa, thus cutting off Berber reinforcements.

ARAGON

At the same time that Leon and Castile were expanding and were driving the Moors out of most of Andalusia, another Christian nation of the peninsula was carrying through a similar development.

In the northeast there had emerged the kingdom of Aragon and, along the Mediterranean shore, the county of Catalonia.   From the southern slopes of the Pyrenees and from the old settlements along the east coast, respectively, Aragon and Catalonia had pushed out the neighboring Moslems and extended their territories in a way generally parallel to the advance of Leon-Castile.   It would seem a reasonable thing to expect that all of these Christian states, including the kingdom of Navarre in the country of the Basques between Castile and Aragon, might have come together to fight their common enemy the Moor and from such a union of purpose might have coalesced into a unified nation.   But the combination of ancient separatist tendencies and of historical differences prevented any such fusion.   Instead the little Christian states were jealous of each other and their inhabitants clung to the local characteristics which marked them off from each other.

Some of those differences are significant.   In the case of the eastern regions the tradition of trading cities and the commercial contacts with the outside world had no counterpart in the remoter lands of the Asturias.

Catalonia also lies at the end of the Pyrenees where passage from north to south is easier than at the western end of that range and consequently there had been constant intercourse with the Frankish lands to the north and a Frankish or French influence which was absent in the west. While in the Asturias and Leon-Castile a civilization had evolved from earlier remnants into a blend of Visigothic aristocratic and Celt-Iberian-Roman democratic elements, in Aragon the organization rested on a quasi-feudal basis in which the chief force was a powerful nobility or essentially Germanic and aristocratic. In the west the towns were stronger than in the east. The kings of Leon-Castile inherited something of the theocratic character of the Visigothic monarchs, while Aragonese kings were creatures of feudal need.

Contemporaneously with Saint Ferdinand's conquests in the south, James the Conqueror, King of Aragon and Count of Catalonia, expelled the Moors from Valencia and carried his frontier to the bounds of the territory Castile had won from Islam. This completed the Reconquest of all the land in the east; what lands remained to the Moslems were in Castile's sphere and Aragon had attained her geographical limits within the peninsula. James the Conqueror launched the eastern kingdoms on another national venture by conquering the island of Majorca. His successors followed this imperialistic lead and from the 13th to the middle of the 15th centuries built up a chain of possessions in the Mediterranean which included the other islands of the Balearic group, Sardinia, Corsica, Sicily, and the Kingdom of Naples. Catalonia also held two little counties of Cerdagne and Roussillon across the Pyrenees on the French side of the mountains. This expansion to the eastward was possible, for one thing, because Aragon had achieved her share of the Crusade and was free to turn her energies to the Mediterranean. As a result the eastern realms were closely in contact with the rest of Europe, were in conflict with the Popes, and were imperial and cosmopolitan in outlook and interests.

CASTILIAN ACTIVITIES

On the other hand Leon-Castile had none of this familiarity with the non-Iberian world. Preoccupied with the century-long task of fighting the infidel, the western kingdom turned her energies inward, developed constitutionally, and kept aloof from interests outside the peninsula. Most notable was the evolution of the *Cortes* or national assembly with delegates from the cities sitting with the privileged estates. Her crusading task left its mark on Castile in the further discouragement of agriculture and the strengthening of the tendency to live in cities where walls offered protection against raiding bands, in the retarding of trade, and in the magnification of the profession of arms.

Save for the unsuccessful ventures into an ambitious foreign policy of Saint Ferdinand's brilliant but impractical son, Alfonso the Learned, the Castilian kings were busied with peninsular activities from the middle of the 13th century to the middle of the 15th. Such local enterprises as efforts to restore authority over the separated land of Portugal, and quarrels over the succession to the throne occupied Castile. Larger in area than either of her neighbors Castile was shut off from the long Iberian coast-lines by Portugal on the west and Aragon on the east, and although her Biscayan and Atlantic ports produced fishing and some shipping, she lagged behind her neighbors in maritime development in the later middle ages. It was in fact by accident that Castile in the 15th century acquired a footing and a claim to that island group of the Canaries which was to be continuously valuable as a way-station on the later voyages across the Atlantic. This archipelago had been known to the ancients, had been visited by a Portuguese expedition in 1341, and in 1344 had been given by the Pope at Avignon to the Castilian prince Luis de la Cerda. The first effective occupation of the islands, however, took place in 1402 when two French adventurers landed and made settlements. Since their resources were inadequate for the subjugation of the natives of all the islands, one of the Frenchmen sailed to Spain and offered to recognize the overlordship of Henry III of Castile in return for help. The Castilian monarch accepted the unexpected gift and notwithstanding counter-claims of Portugal and much shifting of ownership, the islands remained under the suzerainty of the Castilian crown until at the end of the century, Isabella the Catholic brought them under full royal control by purchasing the rights of the current proprietor of part of the islands and by conquering the whole archipelago. With this exception, however, Castile came down to the latter part of the 15th century an insular and aloof state with nothing to match the expanse of overseas possessions of her rival, Aragon.

PORTUGAL—HENRY THE NAVIGATOR

The Iberian country which at this time could show a parallel to Aragon's expansion in the Mediterranean was Portugal, with a good start on her oceanic activity in the Atlantic. In 1385 the Portuguese had won a victory over the Castilians at Aljubarrota which was a guarantee of continued existence independent of their original mother-land Castile, and that battle had begun the career of the vigorous, native, royal house of Avis. King John I of Avis, who had married an English wife, Philippa, the daughter of John of Gaunt and sister of Henry IV of England, began a new era for Portugal. The initial step was the capture of the Moorish stronghold of Ceuta on the southern point of the Straits of Gibraltar; in 1415 John of Avis and his promising sons led a great Portuguese expedition to conquer from the infidel the African key to the Mediterranean. The Ceuta expedition was in keeping with the traditional Iberian interest of the crusade against Islam, it took the place of the medieval tournament for the knighting of the Portuguese princes, the first ceremony in the newly Christianized mosque of Ceuta, and, most significantly, it started Portugal on the path of acquiring territory across the sea and there uniting the tradition of the Christian crusade with the new activity in commerce.

The member of the House of Avis who made the great contribution to Portugal's expansion and to the period of discovery which opened the modern world was the third son of John I, Henry, known by the title of Henry the Navigator (1394-1460). With two brothers between him and the throne this keen-minded prince was free to devote his abundant energies to scientific and maritime endeavor. Henry was a scientist by inclination, and a man of the Renaissance in his desire to experiment and to foster learning, especially in the examination of the geographic mysteries of this earth not yet unveiled to men. But he was also a man of the Iberian middle ages in his interest in crusading and in his patriotic wish to increase the possessions of Portugal. Prince Henry gathered about him men of science and experienced seamen and ship-builders; they worked on theoretical problems of astronomy and geography in Henry's laboratories and on practical developments of ship-construction in the ship-yards of the Navigator Prince near the tip of Cape Saint Vincent. The outcome of this patronage and of Henry's launching of exploring expeditions to put theories into practice aboard his improved ships was that, by the time the prince died in 1460, the Portuguese mariners had discovered the Azores and Cape Verde Islands, had passed one after another of the points on the west coast of Africa which had stood as barriers to sailors of the past, and had voyaged to the Rio Grande in the Gulf of Guinea. The exploration of the western shore of Africa thus fostered was important in widening the bounds of geographic knowledge but much more important for its psychological effect. The old superstitious fears of most European sailors had been the greatest obstacles to venturing out on the ocean. When the ships' companies of Prince Henry on their way down the African coast rounded the cape beyond which it had been believed that the ocean ran over the edge of the earth into space, and returned safely without having been turned black as a mark of God's displeasure, a great victory had been won for human intellectual freedom. Although a temporary lull followed the death of the Navigator, the way he had pointed was to be followed by his countrymen around Africa to the east and the contribution he had made to seafaring was to carry Europeans into the western hemisphere and around the globe.

THE CATHOLIC KINGS

In the year 1469 occurred the marriage of Isabella, Princess of Castile, and Ferdinand the Infante (heir) of Aragon. This marriage was to have far-reaching consequences. Long traditions of hostility separated the two kingdoms; their governmental institutions were distinct in nature and scope, the privileges of their social classes were different, and even commercial intercourse between them was discouraged by tariff barriers. Previous marriages between the reigning houses of the rival states had brought no modification of the long-standing hostility and separatism, but the union of Isabella and Ferdinand was the union of the immediate heirs of the two realms. After a bitter struggle of civil and noble factions in Castile, in the course of which her marriage to the Prince of Aragon was a moving factor, Isabella succeeded her half-brother on the Castilian throne in 1474. Five years later Ferdinand became, by the death of his father, King of Aragon, Count of Catalonia, King of Valencia, and Lord of the imperial territories of the crown of Aragon in the Mediterranean. Thus for the first time in medieval Iberian history the eastern and western halves of the peninsula were brought together by the circumstance that their rulers were husband and wife. The characters of the two rulers were strongly marked and were unusual in that each monarch possessed valuable qualities the other lacked. Isabella was courageous, pious, strong-willed, typically Castilian in her intolerance, in her devotion to the Church, and in her deter-

mination to make her state strong internally. Ferdinand, on the contrary, was the diplomatist and poli-
tician; shrewd, cautious, tight-fisted, a cynic and real-
ist, he had a genius for foreign politics and he inherited
the broad outlook of cosmopolitan Aragon. The joining of the crowns of Castile and Aragon did not mean
an immediate fusion of the two regions or their institutions, but although it was a purely personal union
of the monarchs it marked the beginning of the weld-
ing together of the Spanish kingdoms. The reigns of
the Catholic Kings, as Ferdinand and Isabella were
to be known, also brought about the foundation of the
Spanish Empire across the oceans.

A host of serious problems confronted the Spanish
rulers upon their accession to power. There was first
of all the problem, so familiar in the history of the
15th century, of subduing the turbulent and rebellious nobles and making the monarchy supreme over
faction and baronage. Closely connected with that
pacification and that restoration of royal authority was
the problem of internal development and unification
of the separate regions. There was the task of com-
pleting the traditional crusade by driving out the remnants of the Moors from the peninsula and by meeting
the threatening advance of Islam in the Mediterranean
and North Africa which followed after the Ottoman
Turkish conquest of Constantinople in 1453. And
finally there were many-sided aspects of foreign policy
which the shrewd, active Catholic Kings did not choose
to ignore. Foreign interests began with the opposition of the France of Louis XI and of Portugal to the
marriage of the Kings, and with the Aragonese desire
to recover Cerdagne and Roussillon from French hands
into which they had fallen as securities for aid and

money France had given to Ferdinand's father. Aragon's maritime interests in Sicily and Naples involved Ferdinand and Isabella in the thick of European Renaissance politics in Italy. As their joint reigns wore on, the discovery of the New World and dynastic marriages of their children with the houses of Portugal, of the Hapsburg, and of England, brought still more responsibilities.

ROYAL ABSOLUTISM

Ferdinand and Isabella brought unusual skill and clear-sightedness to bear upon the problem of crushing the nobility. By a combination of adroitness and force they put down disorder and elevated the power of the crown. Just as strong kings were establishing royal despotic authority in England and France out of the chaos introduced by the disintegration of feudalism and of localized political organization, the Catholic Kings built a structure of monarchical absolutism which gave effective government and made the rudiments of a national state. In internal organization the joint rulers of Castile and Aragon created a despotic machinery in the hands of the crown by modifying suitable relics of earlier institutions into efficient royal instruments. An example was the royal council (*Consejo Real*) which previous Kings of Castile had used as an advisory body but which Ferdinand and Isabella enlarged in power to make it the chief cog in their system of absolute government. Another example was the office of *corregidor*, a royal official supervising all local executive and judicial activities, by which the Kings undermined municipal independence and brought the affairs of the old democratic Castilian cities under the control of the throne. In this construction of royal absolutism Ferdinand and Isabella showed genius in refraining from attempting the impossible; in the face of deep-rooted separatism they stopped short of trying to fuse the eastern and western realms which would have resisted bitterly, they concentrated on Castile rather than on Aragon with its tradition of limitation on the crown, and they produced really two sets of despotic government, or what is aptly called a "decentralized despotism." This accomplishment of the Catholic Kings affected the Spanish Empire in two important ways (among others), by making an orderly and royally controlled state which could undertake a great colonial effort and by providing models of administration and political organization for setting up governments for an enormous imperial system under the close control of the crown.

THE KINGS' TRIUMPHS

With sound common sense the Kings set their house in order before attempting anything else, but when they had strengthened their position they achieved resounding triumphs in other spheres. After some ten years of war they brought the historic national task of expelling the infidel to a glorious conclusion by conquering the Kingdom of Granada. On January 2d of the fateful year of 1492 the Catholic Kings received the surrender of Boabdil, the last Emir of Granada, and with the extinction of the last Moorish state in the peninsula the Reconquest was complete. The glory of winning the final victory in the century-long crusade went to Ferdinand and Isabella. They had so conducted the war that it aroused a truly national enthusiasm, they had emphasized the religious note, they had appealed to Christian loyalty so strongly that their subjects acquired for the first time the conspicuous zeal for the faith which became the distinguishing characteristic of the Spaniard, and they had brought to the united rule of Castile and Aragon the prestige of fulfilling the cause initiated at Covadonga. The campaigns before Granada brought to light the talents of Gonsalvo de Cordova, whose military gifts won him the title of the Great Captain, and laid the foundation of that superb Spanish infantry which for a century dominated the battlefields of Europe. Foreign soldiers had flocked to the Spanish standard as mercenaries or as crusading volunteers and upon their return to their homes they spread the reputation of the Kings and their country, giving Europe its first realization that the Spanish kingdoms had become an important factor in world affairs. From a position of insignificance in European currents, this and later political successes of Ferdinand and Isabella raised the Spanish kingdoms within twenty-five years to a place of importance and under their grandson to a place of predominance among the states of the west.

A natural corollary to the conquest of Granada was to complete the territorial unity which that victory consummated by securing unity of race and religion in Iberia. Jews and Moslems had long been tolerated in all parts of Christian Spain, and although some had accepted the cross, large numbers of each group continued in the faith of their fathers. To Isabella's piety such a situation was repugnant, but even worse was the backsliding of many of the converts who had become Christians in form only, while retaining secretly the ways and worship of Judaism or Islam. To hunt out suspected disloyalty among the converts the Kings obtained from the Pope the right to institute a special branch of the court known as the Inquisition which had been an effective means of rooting out heresy in the Church in the middle ages. Far different from the papal Inquisition, however, was the form of that court the Kings set up in their dominions. They placed the supreme control of their Spanish Inquisition in the hands of the crown and made it another instrument for strengthening the absolute power of the monarch. In conjunction with the religious intolerance which the Kings encouraged in the Granada war, the Spanish Inquisition fostered a zealotry which had been absent during the medieval centuries of the Reconquest. The Inquisitorial courts dealt only with those who had gone through the form of conversion to Christianity and, by eradicating apostasy, carried religious unity one step forward.

The next step came out of the victory at Granada; to signalize God's goodness in that triumph some special offering seemed fitting and on the 30th of March, 1492, all the Jews in the Spanish kingdoms were ordered to leave within four months. After that time any Jew found in the land would be subject to the Inquisition since his presence would argue that he must be a convert. Isabella had encouraged the stimulating of religious hatred for years before the edict of expulsion and the process continued against the Moors, to culminate in 1502 in a similar driving out of the Moors from Castile. The economic loss to the kingdoms of the industrious Moorish and Jewish population is a matter of common knowledge. It is also to be observed that it was unfortunate that the coincidence in time of attaining the territorial unity for which patriotic Spaniards had longed with the time of attaining racial unity should have led Spaniards to associate national unity with religious intolerance and to identify the latter with patriotism.[1]

In the field of foreign affairs Ferdinand possessed as marked an interest and a genius as did Isabella in the field of religion, and in foreign policy the reign of the Catholic Kings contributed heavily to the building of the Spanish Empire. A complex and detailed story, Ferdinand's handling of foreign relations was a masterly demonstration of the selfish and immoral politics of the Renaissance. Treacherous and unscrupulous,

[1] The procedure of the Spanish Inquisition, although entirely reasonable from the standpoint of a devout Christian of the 16th century, used secrecy and terror so skilfully as to give the institution its dread efficiency. The Inquisition accepted anonymous denunciation and the accused bore the burden of proving his innocence of such heavy charges as heresy and apostasy. Hence no man could rest secure from the fear of accusation by an enemy or a spy; not even the great ones of the land were immune, for the power of the Inquisitorial court extended over the highest ranks of Spanish society. Contrary to general belief torture was used only to extract evidence or a confession from the accused, never as a punishment. The effort of the Inquisition was to make the accused confess his sin, repent, and be restored to the bosom of the Church after penance. If the accused, found to be a heretic, refused to recant he was "relaxed to the secular arm," that is, handed over to the secular power of the state for punishment. Thus the ecclesiastical body did not shed blood; the Inquisition delivered the heretic to the state with a conventional plea for mercy, which cannot be taken on its face value because it was understood on both sides that the heretic was to be burned at the stake by the secular arm. The public ceremony at which the repentant heretics and the "obstinate" or "relapsed" heretics appeared, the former to make their confessions, the latter to receive their condemnation and punishment, was called the *Auto da Fé,* or "act of faith." Those Moors who accepted Christianity under pressure of the edict of expulsion from Castile were called *Moriscos.* Note that at this time the Moslems were driven out of Castile only, and that professed Moslems were still permitted to remain in the eastern kingdoms.

he combined intrigue, deceit, shady diplomacy, and warfare to secure gains in territory for the Spains, to win alliances, favorable marriages, and diplomatic advantage. In territory Ferdinand augmented Aragon's imperial possessions by recovering the Pyrenean counties of Cerdagne and Roussillon and by gaining the Kingdom of Naples (the southern third of Italy) and added to Castile the formerly independent kingdom of Navarre south of the Pyrenees and a string of fortress towns along the coast of North Africa (although the credit for these last belongs to Isabella and her adviser, Cardinal Ximenes). The marriages the Kings arranged for their five children belong to the sphere of foreign policy and were part and parcel of the great strides in world importance made by the Spanish realms under Ferdinand and Isabella. Of significance to us are the marriage of the Kings' third child and second daughter Joanna to Philip the Handsome, the heir to the lands of the Burgundian and Hapsburg families, and of their youngest child Catherine to the Tudor heir to the English throne, the later Henry VIII. The unpredictable accident of a series of tragic and sudden deaths, however, upset the plans of the Catholic Kings and made Joanna and her Hapsburg son Charles the heirs of Ferdinand and Isabella.

COLUMBUS AND THE DISCOVERIES

The final element in the building of the Spanish Empire under the Catholic Kings was the discovery and settlement of the New World. Since our concern is with beginnings in the formation of a colonial system and an imperial organization by the Kings, we may review briefly the start of the exploring movement.

The immediate background for the discoveries of Columbus was the work of Prince Henry the Navigator, but supplementing the Portuguese pioneering on the Atlantic were the ideas of geography and cosmography the Genoese sailor possessed. The son of a simple weaver of Genoa, Columbus mastered the art of navigation, somehow learned to read Latin and stored his mind with the geographical lore of a number of writers. He pored over a Latin edition of the travels of Marco Polo, the *General History and Geography* of the humanist Æneas Sylvius (later Pope Pius II) and the exhaustive *Image of the World* of Pierre d'Ailly. Not only did he study these works intently but he also collected all bits of information he could reach and checked the written material by the observations of sea-farers. As a young man Columbus went to Portugal, married a relative of one of Prince Henry's captains, took part in Portuguese voyages to Guinea and to England, and carefully noted indications of islands to the west of the groups then known. Thus he combined the observed experience of mariners with past lore and formed his deductions in a scientific way. In d'Ailly's book Columbus noted especially the quotation from Aristotle that "between the end of Spain and the beginning of India the sea was small and navigable in a few days" and the statement from the apocryphal book of Esdras that the earth is six parts land and only one part water. From these sources of information Columbus could have formed the project of reaching Marco Polo's Cathay and Cipango (China and Japan) by sailing westward, without the suggestion contained in the letters of the Florentine doctor Toscanelli, concerning which there is controversy.

Sometime in 1483 Columbus tried to secure aid from John II of Portugal to search for Cipango and the Indies in the western ocean. The King turned the importunate navigator over to a committee of expert cosmographers headed by the Bishop of Ceuta. This body held Columbus's scheme to be futile because it rested on fancy and the descriptions of Marco Polo. In 1484 the Genoese hastily journeyed to Spain and there struggled for seven years to obtain royal assistance for his expedition. Meeting with no encouragement he sent his brother Bartholomew to England to try to interest Henry VII and was himself on the point of giving up his efforts to gain the backing of the Catholic Kings and of departing for France, when Isabella's confessor and Ferdinand's Chancellor of Aragon induced Isabella to lend her aid to the venture.[1]

Curiously enough it was in the military camp at Santa Fé which the Kings had built before Granada during the siege, that the final negotiations and contract between the monarchs and the Admiral were concluded. By that agreement Columbus was given the rank of Admiral in all lands he should discover as well as the right to exercise political authority as viceroy and governor general. The fact that the contract did not confer these rights for exercise in Cipango has been taken as an indication that Columbus expected

[1] On the journey, Bartholomew Columbus fell into the hands of pirates and was so long delayed that when he returned to Spain with the news that the English King had enthusiastically accepted Columbus's scheme, the Discoverer had already sailed westward in the service of the Catholic Kings. Richard Hakluyt, the English chronicler of the voyages of exploration, writes that the pirates were "the occasion why the West Indies were not discovered for England."

to find land in the ocean between Europe and the Far East. The rank of Admiral raised the explorer to the position of a Castilian noble and the title was to be hereditary in his family. In his official position Columbus was to be judge of cases arising from trade with new lands, he was to have one tenth of all products coming thence, and in return for contributing an eighth to the cost of the expedition, he was to share an eighth of the profits. Among other provisions the new Admiral was strictly warned by the Kings to keep away from Portuguese territory in Africa, an early instance of the amicable way the maritime neighbors were to deal with possible conflicts in exploration and settlement. Finally it is to be noted that the popular legend that Ferdinand opposed the venture is doubtful; his officials raised most of the money for the voyage.

After having encountered the severest difficulties in preparation, Columbus's little fleet sailed from Palos on August 3d to make its historic voyage to the New World. The magnificent courage of the Admiral in the face of all obstacles (the mutinous terror of his men and the discouraging failure to strike land within the distance he had expected) is the more admirable when we reflect that he based all his plans on the conviction that there was far less water to cross than proved to be the case. The reward of his steadfastness was the landfall at Watling's Island on October 12, 1492. The account of Columbus's exploration of part of the Cuban shore, of his leaving a settlement at Española (Haiti), of his return to Europe, and of the epoch-making results is generally familiar. The Admiral's three subsequent voyages from 1493 to 1504 and the heart-breaking reverses of fortune which marked his latter years likewise need no detailed repetition. Increasingly dominated by mystic ideas (as evidenced by his plans to revive the Crusades and by his belief that the north shore of South America was the Garden of Eden) and wanting in the practical ability to handle men, Columbus inevitably lost the wide privileges his royal contract gave him and the Kings had to place other men in control of the new lands.

The first breach of the Admiral's monopoly of exploration was the Catholic monarchs' grant to Alonso de Ojeda in 1498 permitting him to carry an expedition westward. Ojeda in 1499 struck the South American coast somewhere near the Guianas and sailed westward and northward to the northernmost point of that continent at Cape de la Vela. Following Ojeda in close succession came the voyages of Niño, Vicente Pinzon (brother of Columbus's invaluable pilot, Martin Pinzon), Diego de Lepe, and Bastidas, up to 1502. Then ensued a lull of six years in exploring activity, to be followed by the conquest of Cuba, the voyage of Pinzon and Diaz de Solis from Honduras along the coast to beyond the eastern point of Brazil, the two abortive attempts to colonize the mainland in 1509 which led to Balboa's discovery of the Pacific and a lasting settlement on Darien isthmus, Ponce de Leon's first visit to Florida, and the voyage of Diaz de Solis direct from Seville to South America. De Solis carried exploration farthest south to the estuary of La Plata in February, 1516 one month after the death of Ferdinand.

PORTUGAL'S EMPIRE

Isabella had died in 1504 and by the passing of her consort in 1516, the end of the reigns of the Catholic

Kings, Spanish captains had skirted the coast-line of the western continents practically all the way from the Plata River to Honduras, had touched at Florida, had discovered the Pacific Ocean, and had explored and settled in the islands of the Caribbean Sea. The Portuguese meanwhile, first in the field and largely by accident deprived of the palm of discovery, had not been idle. John II, the nephew of Prince Henry, upon ascending the throne in 1481, resumed the work of the great Navigator by calling together a committee of scientists to find a means of determining latitude south of the equator where the north star was lost to sight. This committee included the celebrated Martin Behaim and produced a method of finding position at sea by taking the mid-day height of the sun, thus substituting the sextant for the astrolabe which had been used by Europeans since its introduction by the Arabs in the 7th century. Portuguese exploitation of the African coast discovered by the Navigator, especially of the lucrative slave-trade, had continued steadily since his death, but now John II pushed exploration southward from the equatorial region of the Gulf of Guinea. One of his captains, Bartholomew Diaz, was driven in 1486-88 far around the modern Cape of Good Hope in a storm. This rounding of the southern tip of Africa paved the way for the momentous voyage of Vasco da Gama from 1497 to 1499; da Gama circumnavigated Africa and reached the Malabar coast of India (1498), the center of the spice trade in the hands of the Arabs, where he set up a trading station and whence he returned to Portugal with the first cargo of spice to reach Europe directly by sea.

The building of the great Portuguese Empire upon the fabulously rich commerce in spices was the accomplishment of the Marquis of Albuquerque who went to India in 1506 as commander of Portugal's trading posts. With energetic ability and clear-sighted intelligence Albuquerque broke Arab dominance of eastern waters and by 1516 had built up a chain of fortresses and settlements strategically located at the entrances to the Red Sea and the Persian Gulf (the routes of the rival Arab-Venetian spice trade), on the Malabar coast, at Malacca commanding the Malay straits, and in the Spice Islands.

SPANISH EMPIRE AND COLONIAL THEORY

Portugal's early lead in maritime activity had been reflected in papal bulls from the first half of the 15th century granting her in a vague way the lands her mariners might discover, and the first thought of the Catholic Kings upon the return of Columbus from his voyage of 1492 was to secure the Pope's approval of their right to the newly-found land. Although Portugal might claim that Castilian discoveries in the west infringed her monopoly of discovery, the two Iberian rivals peaceably compromised possibly conflicting claims and defined the areas each was to exploit in the Treaty of Tordesillas in 1494.

At the instance of the Catholic Kings, Pope Alexander VI issued four bulls during 1493, conferring full title to the newly discovered lands upon Ferdinand and Isabella. Although the Pope's division of territory between Spain and Portugal had to be readjusted by the Tordesillas Treaty, the papal grants were of great importance in fixing the Spanish theory of title to the New World. This theory is fundamental to an understanding of the colonial system Spain evolved.

Since the new lands were legally Spain's by the Pope's donation, it followed that the natives of those lands were subjects of the King of Castile and therefore Christians. As subjects the natives were to be well-treated, they were considered to have rights at law, and they were to be educated and converted, or in other words, to be given the opportunity to embrace the civilization of the other Castilian subjects. This theory explains the vast difference between the Spanish colonial policy and the English. We must keep this distinction in mind because of our greater familiarity with the colonial theory of the Indians as aliens and enemies rather than as fellow-citizens. In the reign of the Catholic Kings colonial institutions began to appear in an embryonic stage and underlying them all was the conception of the native as a subject of the crown, to be Europeanized rather than to be driven off the land.

Thus the end of the period of the Catholic Kings saw the kingdoms of Castile and Aragon suddenly endowed with the influence and prestige of a great power in European politics. Even though this position was of recent attainment, so substantial had been Ferdinand's success as a diplomat and so imposing his military resources and his territorial possessions in the Mediterranean that the Spanish realms enjoyed a truly imperial position in the Old World. That is to be borne in mind when we consider the Spanish Empire, for it is too easy to think of the Empire only as the discoveries and settlements in the western hemisphere. To the men of the end of the 15th and the early decades of the 16th centuries, moreover, the extent and value of the Spanish lands across the Atlantic were vaguely apprehended whereas the weight of the

European belongings of Castile and Aragon were exactly and respectfully appreciated. The Spanish Indies, as soon as they were proved not to be the desired Indies of the Far East, seemed to be an annoying barrier to the sea-route to the Orient and it was not until the next reign that a more accurate understanding of the potentialities and the riches of those vast lands came to be generally understood in Europe. Yet in both halves of the globe a new empire had been formed from the lands of Castile in Iberia and over the Atlantic (for the Canary Islands and the discoveries in the Indies belonged to the western kingdom) and from the older possessions of Aragon in the Mediterranean and in Iberia. Under the successor of the Catholic Kings we shall see the Empire which had evolved so suddenly from the Spanish realms augmented by the dynastic marriage with the Hapsburgs and provided with an organization and an identity of peculiar meaning to the European world.

CHAPTER II

CHARLES V—THE EMPIRE ESTABLISHED

EFFECTS OF THE CATHOLIC KINGS' DYNASTIC MARRIAGES

ONE of the most astute and momentarily successful phases of the foreign policy of Ferdinand and Isabella had been the dynastic marriages of their children. The Catholic Kings had arranged these marriages to carry forward the work of uniting the peninsula and to increase the international prestige they had created for the Spains; the former object they had attained by a match for their eldest child Isabella with a Portuguese prince and the latter by a double union with the great Hapsburg house.[1] With consummate skill Ferdinand had arranged the marriage of his only son John to Margaret of Hapsburg and of his second daughter Joanna to the Emperor Maximilian's heir Philip the Handsome, the brother of Margaret. Characteristic of Ferdinand's crafty diplomacy had been the extraction of the ultimate political advantage from this Hapsburg alliance, an advantage which he used with telling effect in his long-standing duel with the Valois Kings

[1] The dynastic marriages of the children of the Catholic Kings can be followed by this chart. Affonso of Portugal, to whom Isabella was married in 1490, died a few months after the marriage and she was married to his second cousin, Emmanuel the Fortunate, then reigning in Portugal, in September, 1497. In 1500 Emmanuel married Maria, the fourth child of the Kings. The Kings' youngest child Catherine was married to Arthur Tudor, Prince of Wales, in

of France. But in October, 1497, the brilliant and promising Infante John died suddenly. Soon after, his widow Margaret gave birth to a still-born child and the male line of the Catholic Kings was ended. That left the eldest daughter Isabella, then married to her second Portuguese husband Emmanuel the Fortunate, the apparent successor to the Spanish thrones. Still more tragic disappointment was in store for the Kings; in August, 1498, their daughter Isabella died in childbirth, leaving a baby son Michael as heir to the thrones of Portugal and of the Spains. This baby lived less than two years and upon his death, in 1500, the succession to the crowns of the Catholic Kings had come to their third child Joanna. Inasmuch as Joanna was married to the Archduke Philip, this situation was most distasteful to patriotic Spaniards for it meant that the Spanish titles and rule would pass to the foreign house of Hapsburg after the deaths of Ferdinand and Isabella. On the 24th of February, 1500, a son was born to Joanna, a son who was to become the powerful Charles V. The splendid program

1501. Arthur died a few months later and Catherine was married to his brother, the later Henry VIII of England, after his accession in 1509.

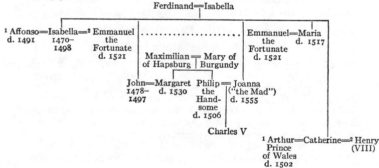

Ferdinand═Isabella

¹ Affonso═Isabella═² Emmanuel .... Emmanuel═Maria
d. 1491   1470–   the   the   d. 1517
          1498   Fortunate   Fortunate
                 d. 1521   d. 1521
                        Maximilian ═ Mary of
                        of Hapsburg Burgundy

                        John═Margaret Philip ═ Joanna
                        1478– d. 1530 the   ("the Mad")
                        1497   Hand- d. 1555
                                      some
                                      d. 1506

                              Charles V

                                        ¹ Arthur═Catherine═² Henry
                                        Prince   (VIII)
                                        of Wales
                                        d. 1502

of consolidating the Iberian states and of bringing them into the front rank of European powers had advanced materially under the clever activity of the Catholic Kings but all their triumphs had turned bitter. The tragic series of deaths among their children meant that now all the efforts of the Catholic monarchs would go to swell the already enormous possessions of the "marrying" Hapsburg family and that their labors had improved a state which would finally become merely a province among the lands of a non-Iberian, alien German house.

When he was only a few months old, therefore, Joanna's son Charles was the ultimate heir to the territories of the Catholic Kings (the baby Michael did not die until after Charles was born). More than that, the tiny prince was the apparent inheritor of the patrimony of the Hapsburgs in and about Austria, of the extra-legal but strong customary claim of that house to the elected dignity of Holy Roman Emperor, and of the vast lands of the Dukes of Burgundy (through his father's mother, Mary of Burgundy, daughter and heiress of Charles the Bold), the Low Countries, northeastern France, Luxemburg, Franche Comté, and other scattered holdings. In all this array of dynastic possessions no one in his senses could imagine that Castile and Aragon would receive paramount attention or even bare consideration for their peculiar interests, and the Kings could look ahead to a gloomy future in which their beloved kingdoms would be subordinate elements in the trans-Pyrenean domains of a foreign monarch. Intensifying the foreignness of the new heir was the fact that Charles, born at Ghent, was brought up entirely in the Netherlands by Flemish tutors and guardians. From the time he was four years old until he was seventeen he did not see his mother. Upon the death of Isabella in 1504 Joanna and Philip had journeyed to Spain to receive Castile in succession to Isabella; Philip died there in 1506, and Joanna, her unstable mind unsettled by these losses so that from this time she was known as "the Mad," remained in Castile for the rest of her life. Thus no Spanish influence entered into the upbringing of Charles, who grew to young manhood a Fleming of the Flemings.

In January, 1516, Ferdinand died, and, in spite of his various intricate manœuvres to offset the Hapsburg control of the Spains, the Catholic King left his Aragonese lands to his grandson Charles. This was in accordance with Spanish law which established primogeniture in royal inheritance. By that time Charles was already joint ruler of Castile with his mother, although her generally known mental incapacity left Charles practically sole sovereign; her inclusion in the title was a bit of face-saving by the Castilians, who cordially hated the foreigner, as had their medieval forefathers. Until the young king should arrive from the Low Countries the aged Cardinal Ximenes acted as regent in Castile and showed the same iron qualities which he had exhibited in crushing Islam in Granada and in pushing the conquest of Moorish fortified cities in North Africa. It was thanks to the octogenarian Cardinal that when Charles of Ghent reached his Iberian dominions in 1517, he found the royal authority firm; the nobles had made a last effort to seize power upon the death of Ferdinand but had been unable to make headway against the regent. The delay of the new king in coming to Spain arose from sound reasons; he had serious troubles on his

hands in the Netherlands and he had to make sure
of good relations with France before it was safe to
journey to Spain. The intensely proud and self-cen-
tered Castilians, however, with all their old insularity
and localism, could not appreciate these reasons and
they saw only an insulting reluctance in his tarrying
in the north. Consequently the Spaniards as a whole
awaited their new monarch with gloomy forebodings
and when Charles finally landed at Villaviciosa in October, 1517, and began a slow progress through Castile
the forebodings seemed confirmed. For the king appeared unprepossessing, he was hesitant of speech, he
knew no Spanish and spoke only French and Flemish,
and, worst of all, he was accompanied by a train of
some five hundred elegant Burgundian courtiers and
ministers. At every turn these foreigners angered and
exasperated the haughty Castilians. The Flemings
were luxurious and gorgeous worldlings whose con-
tempt for the simple state of the ruder Spanish aristoc-
racy wounded the social and national pride of the latter; the northerners were rapacious in their efforts to
secure rich pensions and dignities in the Spanish political and ecclesiastical organization. It was almost un-
bearably galling to Castilians that their new ruler
should have such hateful followers; that he should
accept their domination and should lean upon them for
advice, drove the Spaniards to fury.

ACCESSION OF CHARLES V

In January, 1518, the Cortes of Castile assembled at
Valladolid to swear allegiance to the new sovereign.
With characteristic frankness the delegates protested
against the presence of foreigners, told the king that

the realm should not be impoverished for the benefit of favorites and aliens, criticized his inability to speak Spanish, referred to him as "Your Highness" in the old Spanish fashion instead of as "Your Majesty" which Charles preferred, and named his mother Joanna specifically as joint ruler.[1] Charles secured a subsidy of 600,000 ducats and then proceeded to Saragossa to secure the recognition of the Cortes of Aragon. Here he encountered similar opposition, particularly when it came to getting the grant of money Charles wished the Cortes to vote him. It had become known by this time that the Emperor Maximilian, the king's Hapsburg grandfather, had not long to live and it behoved Charles to start his campaign of bribery of the imperial electors to secure his election as Emperor. The Aragonese were stubborn, however, and the king was obliged to remain until the end of January, 1519, before he could obtain Aragon's recognition and a modest grant of 200,000 ducats. He next journeyed to Barcelona for the Catalan Cortes's recognition and although the Catalans were so determined not to be victimized by the Flemings that they turned the tables and fleeced the foreigners, the royal affairs went more smoothly than in the two preceding meetings of Castile and Aragon.

But on the way to Catalonia news reached Charles that his grandfather was dead and he was eager to get to Germany to look after his political inter-

[1] Joanna was placed ahead of Charles in official designation. As King of Castile, King of Aragon, King of Valencia, Count of Catalonia, and so on, Charles was officially "Charles I," since no other ruler of that name had ever occupied the Spanish thrones. But in the position of Holy Roman Emperor, Charles was the fifth of the name and it is by his title of "Charles V" that he is most commonly known, in Spain as well as elsewhere.

ests there. In haste to get away from Spain, the king cancelled his visit to Valencia, sending a proxy to secure the allegiance of the Cortes of that kingdom, and summoned the Cortes of Castile to meet him at Santiago de Compostela. This was a most unusual procedure. The Castilian Cortes had been accustomed to meet in one of the great towns of Old or New Castile in central Iberia and Castilian opinion disliked the idea of calling the Cortes to the far northwestern region of Galicia, near to the Atlantic ports. After encountering the stiff opposition of that body Charles adjourned the Cortes to the port of Corunna and by a mixture of bribery and intimidation wrung from the assembly the vote of additional money. He embarked hastily for the Low Countries on May 20, 1520. On the eve of sailing Charles proclaimed as regent in his absence his former tutor, Adrian of Utrecht. Although he imposed restrictions on the regent's power designed to salve Spanish feelings, the king's action further angered his subjects for he had promised the contrary; in breaking his word Charles had undone the favorable impression of the last few months.

Meantime the attention of Europe had been directed to the contest for the imperial election, in which the ability of Charles's backers to continue the sordid bribery of the Electors longer than his French rival, had given the young Hapsburg the dignity of Holy Roman Emperor over the active candidacy of Francis I of France and the tentative candidacy of Henry VIII of England. Charles excused his departure from Spain by citing the necessity (according to the Golden Bull of 1356) of ratifying his election by the ceremony of coronation; on October 23, 1520, he was crowned King of the Romans at Charlemagne's old capital of Aix-la-Chapelle and from that time was legally entitled "Emperor Elect." In addition to the traditional medieval office of Emperor of the Holy Roman Empire Charles V at this time united under his personal sway an unprecedentedly vast expanse of territory and political power. From his Spanish grandparents he possessed the Spanish realms of Castile, Navarre, Aragon, Catalonia, and Valencia, the old Aragonese imperial lands of Cerdagne and Roussillon across the Pyrenees, the Balearics, Sardinia, the kingdoms of Sicily and of Naples, and the more recently acquired Castilian holdings of the Canaries and the New World, as well as the Spanish conquests of North African fortress cities. The successor of the Catholic Kings could add to the extensive lands of their old and new empires, wide territories inherited from his paternal grandparents. These comprised the Burgundian possessions of Charles's father's mother, Mary of Burgundy, which included Flanders and Artois in northeastern France, Franche Comté and Charolais in eastern France, Luxemburg and a host of small states making up the Low Countries. Also Charles had inherited from his paternal grandfather Maximilian, the Hapsburg patrimony of Austria, Carinthia, Carniola, Styria, Tyrol and scattered Swiss holdings, lands on the upper Rhine, and a claim to the Duchy of Milan in Italy. No ruler in European history had headed so enormous an extent of territory, yet the magnitude of Charles's empire was to be increased during his reign by discovery and conquest beyond the seas. To Spain, however, the grandiose power of her new king meant little; the old separatist isolation from the rest of the world and the old hatred of the foreigner conspired to leave the impression with the Spaniards that their king left the peninsula in 1520 merely because he preferred Germany to Spain; and they might have remained un-reconciled to the fact that their king was busying him-self in affairs across the Pyrenees had not an event occurred in Germany which also touched the closest interest of Spaniards.

SPAIN'S NEW COURSE

That event was the religious revolt of Martin Luther and the beginning of the Protestant Reformation. Fol-lowing his coronation Charles had summoned his first Imperial Diet to meet at Worms in the spring of 1521 and at that memorable meeting he had called Luther before the assemblage of the great ones of the Empire and had denounced the Saxon monk's attack on the Church. Hating heresy and hating still more anything which savored of rebellion against constituted author-ity, Charles outlawed the entire reform movement and made it clear that he should exert his whole strength to defend the fabric of the old Roman Catholic faith. Nothing the Emperor could have done would have aroused greater enthusiasm among his Spanish subjects. Since the Catholic Kings had joined to the medieval tradition of defending the Christian cause the newer tradition of fanatical zeal for the Church, the Span-iards had been the most loyal western Christians; they had detested heresy and they longed to see the Lu-theran movement crushed. If their king were to use his international position to defend the Church against heretical attack they would give him hearty support and if his outside responsibilities included the glorious duty of championing the faith, they were ready to ap-prove his activities outside the peninsula. This religious element put a final touch on the process of imperial and international education of the Spanish people, especially the portion of the population in the interior of Spain which had lacked the Catalonian and Aragonese experience in expansion, trade and foreign dominion in the past. From this time Spaniards became continentally minded and imperially minded, accepting the idea that it was their national destiny to hold an empire and to play a large part in the European affairs of which they had for centuries been distant and aloof spectators.

The dawning of interest in the imperial opportunities opening before their king and the Spaniards' belated acceptance of the situation came at about the time Charles returned to the peninsula in 1522; in the meantime his authority had been threatened by revolt. The bad impression the young monarch and his foreign train had made upon his Spanish subjects was intensified by the manner of his departure and by his dealings with the Castilian Cortes at Santiago and Corunna. So violent was the opposition that the representatives (*procuradores*) of the Castilian towns were denounced and roughly handled by their constituents, and the *procuradores* of Segovia were hanged by a mob because the Cortes had voted a grant of money to the king who was going away from Spain. The discontent in Castile soon flared up in a rising against the king's regent and the movement, starting in the towns and at first enlisting support from all classes, rapidly became a revolution of dangerous proportions. From the practice of proclaiming a commune or *Comunidad* to govern the cities from which the rebels expelled the royal officers, the revolt has been called the *Comunero* movement. After a promising start the old class separatism weakened the solidarity of the *Comuneros* by causing the withdrawal of most of the nobles, and the delay of the leaders and the conservative fears that the revolt would go too far in the direction of democracy combined to defeat the revolution. Its two years of activity came to an end in 1521 and left the royal power stronger than it had been before.

While the *Comunero* revolt was in progress a somewhat similar revolution was raging in Valencia. In that kingdom there had been bad feeling since Charles had slighted the realm by failing to appear in person for recognition and out of this resentment grew an uprising known as the *Germanía* revolt which rapidly developed into a class-war between the third estate and the privileged orders. Adrian of Utrecht mistook the nature of the struggle at the outset and sent aid to the commoners, but later discovered his mistake and despatched royal forces to help the nobles put down the insurrection. Another evidence of the traditional separatism is that the two revolts were unable to join hands or coöperate with each other in spite of their common aims. The *Germanía* was in its last stages when Charles came back to Spain and an ultimate effect of the revolt was the expulsion of the Moors from all the eastern regions some years later (completed by January 1, 1526).

INTERNAL GOVERNMENT

From 1522 on Charles was never again to encounter opposition or hostility from Spaniards, for his second visit to the peninsula marked the beginning of mutual appreciation and affection between king and subjects. In addition to the changed attitude of Spain toward the

Emperor-King's external responsibilities, Spain saw in him a more prepossessing person. Charles had been slow in maturing but now, in 1522, he had grown into a distinguished and strong man; he showed decision and independent judgment, he no longer leaned on Flemish councillors, and instead of Burgundian courtiers he brought with him a force of 4,000 German *landsknechts* and a park of artillery. Moreover, Charles had begun to understand his Iberian realms and people better; a process of Hispanicization of the Hapsburg commenced to operate. He learned Spanish, grew more and more fond of the land, married an Iberian, Isabella of Portugal, and spent a total of sixteen years of his reign of forty in Spain, longer than he spent in any other part of his dominions after 1516. At the end of his career it was to Spain that Charles retired to end his days, and his beloved son Philip was brought up in Spain as a Spaniard of the Spaniards.

In handling internal affairs in his Iberian kingdoms Charles carried the unification of the separate parts somewhat further than his grandparents but he did not bring about a complete or definitive union of the kingdoms. For one thing he did represent a personal union hitherto absent, for he united in his person the titles of all the Iberian states but Portugal. But the force of the past was too strong to bring about an extinction of separate institutions; Charles wisely refrained from trying too much, and his government was a "de-centralized despotism" like that of the Catholic Kings. Like them he utilized the Councils as effective instruments for absolute administration and even carried their development further, adding new groups and regulating conciliar powers. One consequence of the magnitude of the European dominions of the Emperor was that he was called away from the peninsula often and in his absences the old Council of Castile (the *Consejo Real* of Ferdinand and Isabella) had an opportunity to exercise increased responsibility. Other councils created or developed by Charles included the Council of State (*Consejo de Estado*) which was rather a figure-head body concerned with foreign affairs and made up of nobles who were kept out of mischief by the formal gesture of membership in this council. Among several other Councils were the old Council of Aragon, and a new Privy Council (*Consejo Privado*) to assist the regents of Flanders in governing the Low Countries. The *Suprema* continued to be the strong directing body for the Inquisition as of old. Another new creation of Charles's reign was a colonial body, the Council of the Indies (*Consejo de las Indias*), to be considered later in connection with the colonial system.

Overshadowing all others in power and importance was the Council of Castile; but although it was the mightiest of the conciliar bodies and wielded greatest authority in internal affairs, even this council remained a docile servant of the crown with slight chance to assert itself against the throne or to menace the King's unchecked power. Under Charles the councils (save for the *Consejo de Estado*) were chiefly manned by *letrados*, or trained lawyers, and experienced men of affairs from the Third Estate. These men, as in other centralized royal absolute states of western Europe, owed everything to the King, and could be counted on to obey the royal instructions. Charles feared strong and independent advisers; the lesson of the middle ages that monarchs suffered at the hands of masterful, domineering nobles had made an impression on Charles and he filled his councils with tenacious, hard-working, but unoriginal men, preferring "docility to leadership" and sacrificing initiative to loyal obedience. The fruits of the Emperor's political sagacity are embodied in the instructions he left to his son Philip, and in these he urged his successor to avoid letting one councillor become more powerful than the rest, lest the King lose his complete mastery of the government by depending too much on a brilliant or dominating minister.[1]

At the same time that the Councils gained in strength and put into execution the royal absolutism in Spain the oldest auxiliary political institution of the kingdoms lost ground. The Cortes had decreased in importance in the 15th century and had fallen behind still more during the reigns of the Catholic Kings. In Castile particularly, the old popular body had numbered only the representatives of the traditional eighteen Castilian towns. The weakened political authority of the Cortes was reflected in the fact that it had become merely a tax-voting body and inasmuch as the upper orders of clergy and nobility were exempt from paying taxes they had stopped attending Cortes, both because they were uninterested and because it would have been a confession of social degradation to be associated with *pecheros* (tax-payers).

[1] An interesting parallel to Charles's use of conciliar institutions was the contemporary utilization of Councils to secure effective and absolute royal government by the Tudor kings in England. Another striking example of a monarch's governing by councils was to be furnished in the succeeding century by Louis XIV of France. Louis, in close touch with Spain since his mother and his wife were Spanish princesses, drew on Spanish Hapsburg practice for his councils and for the elaborate court etiquette he installed at Versailles.

For several reasons Charles was desirous of remedying this situation. On the one hand the Emperor was always in need of money; if he could devise a way to secure taxes or money contributions from the privileged orders it would help relieve his chronic poverty. Another consideration was that nobles and clerics failed to play their part in the deliberations on Castilian affairs and should be brought back to active participation in Cortes. Another point was that the Emperor seems to have had an intention of paving the way for a union of institutions of the eastern and western kingdoms some day, and to bring about such a fusion it would first be necessary to bring the political bodies of the regions into some sort of harmony. In Aragon the Cortes retained more of its ancient vigor and had a greater attendance of prelates and lords, so that the upper groups of Castile would have to be brought back to their Cortes to make it more nearly akin to Aragon's in practice. Charles made several efforts to reform the Castilian Cortes, notably in 1538 when he commanded attendance of all the orders and proposed changes in the tax system which would have placed an indirect tax on food in place of the multitude of direct taxes borne by the lower class. In return for the tax reform the Emperor offered to give increased powers to the Cortes. The deputies were too strongly steeped in the caste and separatist traditions of Castile to realize the advantage to all subjects in making a genuine parliamentary body with rights of control or limitation on the crown, and the upper estates defeated the project. Consequently the Cortes fell further into the background as a vital political factor, and that splendid beginning of a democratic system which the past had shaped in Castile from Roman and Iberian elements failed in the national sphere and remained alive only in the cities and in the tradition of municipal democracy.

Economically the reign of Charles V started the Spains on the way to a decline which Spaniards heroically staved off but which overtook the nation in the next century. Ironically enough that reign saw the streams of bullion from the New World pouring into Iberia in the 1540s and 1550s, so that the world at large looked upon the fortunate peninsula as Hesperides in very truth. Yet in spite of the treasure from Mexican and Peruvian mines Spain was pinched and badly off materially. Buying most of her food supply and her manufactured goods from outside and exporting chiefly soldiers and priests, the precious metals tended to flow across the Pyrenees. The great source of economic distress, however, lay in the responsibilities and necessities of her Hapsburg sovereign. Charles was forced to find huge sums of money to carry on the great undertakings of governing his widespread territories and of fighting wars in every corner of western Europe and the Mediterranean. Spain alone of all his lands could supply a great sum, the Emperor had no means of extracting money from Germany or Italy, and throughout his reign and that of his son, Spain furnished the monarch with the lion's share of the money and men he employed in war and diplomacy. This expenditure was too heavy a burden for regions only recently arrived at the status of a European power, especially for regions so largely made up of uncommercial and non-industrial population as the inland Iberian districts. Charles aggravated the situation by measures to produce immediate revenue which were unsound economically.   But the backbone of the difficulty was that the Spanish realms had to shoulder expenditures too heavy for them, burdens they bore willingly enough since they saw that much of the Emperor's effort was going to crush the Lutheran heresy and the might of Islam on the sea and in North Africa.   It seems to us at this distance of time a tragic thing that so many of the sons of Spain should have been called away to continental scenes of action at a time when the New World lay newly opened for Castilian activity and when the Indies could have used every soul who could leave the peninsula.   The economic weakness of the kingdoms at the end of Charles's reign, however, was not apparent to contemporaries, and the impression of boundless wealth in Spanish hands persisted for generations as a universal belief.

FOREIGN AFFAIRS—FRANCE

The external problems of the Hapsburg King of the Spains were of the utmost complexity and variety. Purely from the Spanish side his foreign relations were bound to be complicated and grave, for the empire he had inherited from Ferdinand and Isabella in the Old World involved rivalry with France and participation in general continental diplomacy.   In addition to these Spanish interests Charles must encounter opposition and even greater international activity arising from the interests of his paternal inheritance, the Burgundian-Hapsburg empire.   The third great division of Charles's imperial possessions, the lands in the New World, belonged by itself and in that monarch's time remained rather outside the current of continental European politics; it did not affect seriously international problems until the period of the next Spanish king, Philip II. External European affairs had engaged the attention of Charles V before he had set foot in the Iberian peninsula and all through his eventful career they were always pressing and always demanding a large share of his effort. France from the start was an enemy; there were many reasons for this hostility. Politically, the quarrel of Louis XI and Charles the Bold of Burgundy, the latter the great-grandfather of Charles V, continued in the Valois desire to add Franche Comté to the French royal domain and in Charles's wish to recover the Duchy of Burgundy which Charles the Bold had lost to the French King. In Italy the Hapsburg suzerainty over the Duchy of Milan clashed with the ambitions of Francis I of France to hold that trans-Alpine duchy. The triumphs of Ferdinand the Catholic in gaining the Kingdom of Naples, the Kingdom of Navarre, and the counties of Cerdagne and Roussillon bequeathed to Charles another cause of dispute with his neighbor, since Francis I might hope to reverse the defeats his predecessors had suffered in those regions by taking them from Charles. Geography came into play when Charles gained the crowns of Spain because he then held lands on two sides of France, the Netherlands to the northeast and east, and Spain to the south. Then in 1519 this "encirclement" of France became aggravated by Charles's election to the imperial dignity, for then France was caught between two fires in earnest. That was the reason that war between Hapsburg and Valois became inevitable as soon as Charles had come into all his political and territorial inheritance. The safety of the French dynasty of the Valois was threatened by the preponderance of the Hapsburg holdings; as a result family or dynastic wars on an international scale appeared in European history to remain the leading factor in international relations for generations to come.

HAPSBURG-VALOIS WARS AND THE BALANCE OF POWER

In addition to France, Charles V had two other constant and inveterate enemies, the Protestants in the Holy Roman Empire and the Turks in the Mediterranean basin and in the Danube valley. Against these three foes the Emperor labored to build up alliances, to concentrate diplomatic and military strength, and to carry on warfare, and around these struggles the history of Europe in the first half of the 16th century turned. At the outset Charles had the support of Henry VIII of England, of several of the Italian princes, and of the Pope; he had the advantage of the veteran Spanish army, which the Great Captain, Gonsalvo de Cordova, had organized and led victoriously in Ferdinand's Italian wars. From 1521 until his abdication in 1556 Charles fought and concluded four wars with France and began a fifth which he left in progress, wars which are known as "Hapsburg-Valois Wars" from the dynasties involved. Although the Emperor started the duel with so heavily predominant power that he appeared certain to defeat his French rival and dismember the French kingdom, he was forced at the end of the fourth war (by the Peace of Crespy, 1544) to be content with a draw, with neither side securing any territorial gain. The wars were marked by Charles's victory at Pavia in 1525 in which his army not only crushed the French but actually took the French King Francis a prisoner, by the sack of

Rome by the Imperialist-Spanish army in 1527 which made the Pope a captive in the hands of Charles's forces, and by the emergence of the international principle of the Balance of Power. For it was the fear that Charles's success would make him so overwhelmingly powerful that he would menace the safety of all other European states which led England to withdraw from alliance with the Emperor and which made states trust their security to the doctrine of balanced strength against too great a concentration of power in the hands of any one state. The Balance of Power principle did not emerge as a clearly appreciated maxim at this time but the germ of it came out of this situation.

Another consequence of the Emperor's French wars was the extension of Spanish domination in Italy. Following the lead of Ferdinand the Catholic in gaining Naples, Charles secured the Duchy of Milan as the fruit of his victory over Francis I at Pavia. Thus firmly established in key-positions in the northern and southern ends of the peninsula, Spanish influence extended during the reign over Florence, Siena, Savoy, Genoa and several smaller principalities. This influence existed in the form of alliances, marriage relationships, overlordship, or outright possession and military control. The exact political situation in these Italian states makes an involved story, but two factors are conspicuous. One is that Milan ultimately became a full Spanish possession by the gift of the Emperor to his son Philip. The other is that from the time of the first Hapsburg-Valois War the century-long suzerainty of the Holy Roman Emperor over the lands of Italy began to give way to Spain's ascendancy. In settling Italian problems Charles inclined toward the Iberian rather than the Hapsburg interest and at the end of his reign he left the greater part of the Italian peninsula virtually dependent on the Spanish Empire.

THE REFORMATION

From the Spanish angle the Hapsburg-Valois wars were less popular than hostilities against the Emperor's other two enemies. The Castilian Cortes constantly petitioned in its *cuadernos* that the King "make peace with Christian kings" and turn his arms against the heretic and the infidel. There speaks the medieval Spanish spirit, and since the money and the bulk of the men Charles was using in his wars were coming from Spain the country had a right to speak. But the medieval spirit was on the wane in the world of the 16th century; as evidence, Charles's army had attacked the papal city. Likewise, Francis I (who bore the proud title of the French Kings of the middle ages of "The Most Christian King"), after his disastrous defeat at Pavia, had made an alliance with the Turkish Sultan against the Emperor, and both Francis I and his successor Henry II, who persecuted Protestants in their own dominions, entered into close alliance with the Lutheran princes in Germany to make trouble for Charles V. Religious considerations became secondary to political and Charles himself, who was decently pious and who wished to put down the heresy in Germany, would not jeopardize political interests for the sake of religion. In dealing with Luther's revolt against the Church, Charles was dealing with a matter affecting the internal control of one of his possessions and there constitutional and local German considerations entered into the situation. Save for the person of Charles as ruler, Catholicism had been the one element common to all his dominions.   Moreover, the multitude of burdens and problems confronting the Emperor prevented him from devoting all his energies to any one problem and the pressure of such cares as the French wars and the campaigns against the Turk kept him from concentrating his attention on the Lutherans until after 1544. At his first Diet at Worms Charles had leveled the official condemnation of the imperial ban upon the religious revolution, to the satisfaction of Spain, but he could not spare the time to enforce it and until the latter part of his reign, he tried to bring about some compromise between Protestant and Catholic parties. Meanwhile the Lutheran movement gained sufficient strength to defeat all attempts to crush it by force and the Protestant princes defended their cause by allying with the Emperor's foes.   At the end of a long struggle Protestantism won the right to continued existence in the Holy Roman Empire.

TURKS AND CORSAIRS

The third constant enemy touched Spain more directly than Lutheran or Frenchman.   Because of her experience with the Moslem at home and her centuries of the Reconquest Spain felt an interest in the condition of North Africa and the Mediterranean Sea.   Her maritime commerce to the eastward had for long been subject to piratical raids by Moorish corsairs who found good hiding-places in the rocky Barbary coast from Morocco to Tunis.[1]   Spanish interests in the Moslem region across the water to the southward had

---

[1] The word *corsair* means a summer campaign and indicates the characteristic raiding of commerce by the North African pirates during good weather.

also been increased by the offensive launched under the initiative of Cardinal Ximenes, in the preceding reign, which had yielded the conquest of several fortified ports. The presence in North Africa of Moors driven out of Castile and the Aragonese realms concerned Spaniards, since those exiles stirred their coreligionists to plundering attacks on Spanish coasts and shipping. Another stimulus to activity against Islam came from the rise to importance of the Ottoman Turks who had in 1453 driven out the eastern defender of Europe and planted their expanding power at Constantinople to menace the Christian west. The Turkish Empire under its greatest Sultan, Suleiman (II) the Magnificent, was a threat to Europe in two quarters; overland the Turks had begun to march up the Danube to attack the Hapsburg lands from the east, and by sea they were advancing through the Levant and challenging Christian sea-power. In the latter direction the Turks struck at the old Aragonese Empire, both its lines of trade and communication with Naples and Sicily by water, and southern Italy itself (Greece, Epirus, Albania, and lower Dalmatia across the Straits of Otranto and the Adriatic were already in the possession of the Ottomans) and the eastern Spanish kingdoms were concerned thereby. The rejuvenation of Islam's offensive by the upcoming Turks came home even more closely to Spain in the early years of Charles's reign when the independent local rulers of the small Moorish states of North Africa were driven by their fear of further Spanish attack and expansion to acknowledge the Ottoman Sultan as their overlord and to place themselves under his protection.[1] Besides these fac-

[1] The single important exception was the ruler of Morocco who maintained an independent power as "Emperor." In religion even

tors peculiarly influencing his Spanish subjects to desire war on the infidel, Charles was concerned in his capacity as head of the Hapsburg house and as Holy Roman Emperor to block the invasion of Austrian lands and the blow at Europe from the east. For him too the Turkish problem was complicated by the fact that his Valois enemy had allied with Suleiman after Pavia.[1]

For these various reasons the conflicts with the Moslem were vital concerns of the Emperor and of his Spanish kingdoms. The connection between the Barbary pirates and the Ottoman Empire made an effective offensive combination; the Turks have always been notorious for their maritime weakness while the North

he acknowledged the authority of the Sultan as Caliph, a dignity the Turk had seized by the conquest of Mecca in 1517.

[1] In desperation at his defeat and capture by Charles's forces at Pavia, Francis I had opened negotiations with the Sultan for a Franco-Turkish alliance against the Emperor. The following letter is a reply from Suleiman to this request:

"He [God] is the elevated, the rich, the generous, the helpful. I, who am by the grace of that One whose power is glorified and whose word is exalted by the sacred miracles of Mohammed (upon whom be the benediction of God and the praise!), sun of the heaven of prophecy, star of the constellation of the apostles, chief of the army of prophets, guide of the cohort of the elect, by the coöperation of the sainted souls of his four friends Abu-Bekr, Omar, Osman, and Ali (may the satisfaction of the Most-High be on all of them!) as well as all the favorites of God; I, I say, who am the Sultan of Sultans, the sovereign of sovereigns, the dispenser of crowns to the monarchs of the surface of the globe, the shadow of God on earth, the Sultan and Padishah of the White Sea, of the Black Sea, of Roumelia, of Anatolia, of Caramania, of the land of Roum [Rome], of Zulcadria, of Diarbekr, of Kurdistan, of Azerbaijan, of Persia, of Damascus, of Aleppo, of Cairo, of Mecca, of Medina, of Jerusalem, of all Arabia, of the Yemen, and of many other countries which my noble grandfathers and my illustrious ancestors (may God illumine their tombs!) conquered by the force of their arms, and

African Berbers were skilful and daring sailors and sea-fighters. From the Barbary region Suleiman secured an admiral for the first regular Turkish navy of consequence by enticing into his service the pirate Kheir-ed-Din, who had made himself master of Algiers and had built up a thriving corsair fleet.[1] With the approval and encouragement of the Spanish realms, Charles waged intermittent warfare against Turks and Barbary pirates. Part of the struggle lay in the Danube Valley and was straight land warfare, in which

which my august majesty has equally conquered with my shining sword and my victorious blade, Sultan Suleiman-Khan, son of Sultan Selim-Khan, son of Sultan Bayezid-Khan:

"To thee, Francis, King of the land of France:

"Thou hast sent a letter to my Porte, asylum of sovereigns, by thy faithful agent Frangipani, thou hast also given him sundry verbal messages. Thou hast made known that thine enemy hath seized thy country, and that thou art actually in prison, and thou hast asked aid here and help for thy deliverance. Everything thou hast said having been exposed at the foot of my throne, refuge of the world, my imperial knowledge has embraced it in detail and I have made complete understanding of it.

"It is not astonishing that emperors should be defeated and become prisoners. Take courage then and be not humbled. Our glorious ancestors and illustrious forefathers (may God illumine their tombs!) never ceased to make war to repulse the enemy and conquer countries. We also have followed in their path. We have conquered at all times, provinces and citadels, strong and difficult of access. Night and day our horse is saddled and our sabre is belted on.

"May God on high help the good! To whatever object His wish attaches, may it be carried out! For the rest, in asking thine ambassador, thou wilt be informed. Know it thus!

"Written at the beginning of the moon of Reibul-Akhir, 932 [1526 A.D.], at the residence of the capital of the Empire, Constantinople the well-supplied and the well-guarded." (Charrière, *Négociations du Levant*, I, 116-118.)

[1] Kheir-ed-Din was commonly known to the west as Barbarossa. His elder brother Arudj, who wore a red beard and who was the original bearer of the nickname (Barba-rossa means red-beard), came from their native Ægean island with a modest following of

the Emperor generally stood on the defensive as in the repulse of Suleiman's siege of Vienna in 1529. But the greater part of the conflict lay on the sea and the North African coast. Without following the operations in detail the high points may be noted. In 1535 Charles gained his outstanding success by capturing Tunis in a joint land and naval attack at which the Emperor was present. The Christian forces, however, were driven off in a similar attempt on Algiers in 1541, and were credited with a defeat in a great sea-fight off Prevesa in 1538, where the imperial admiral, the Genoese Andrea Doria, encountered Barbarossa at the head of the Turkish navy. These naval wars ran steadily throughout the reign and marked an apogee in the development of galley-fighting. As a whole the wars with the infidel saw no permanent gains for Christian arms and as far as Spain was concerned they brought a loss of influence and control in North Africa. They did, however, create Spanish naval power in the Mediterranean and establish a Spanish naval tradition based on the use of the galley, the typical fighting-ship of that tideless sea ever since classic antiquity.

THE TWO EMPIRES—OLD AND NEW WORLD

Of transcendent importance in the history of the group of imperial possessions which made up the Em-

pirates and a few small galleys to establish a foothold at Algiers in 1512. Arudj cowed neighboring Moorish Emirs and made Algiers a corsair center. Upon his death in action, his younger brother Kheir-ed-Din succeeded to his control of the pirate nest and to his appellation of Barbarossa, in spite of the fact that Kheir-ed-Din's beard was black. These Mediterranean sea-rovers are not to be confused with the 12th century Holy Roman Emperor, Frederick I, who was also known as Barbarossa from the color of his beard.

pire of Charles, the First and the Fifth, is the imperial domain of Castile across the Atlantic, the New World colonies. Here is another portion of his inheritance which was purely Spanish in origin and the foundations of which belonged to the tale of accomplishments of the Catholic Kings. At this point it is well to bear in mind that although for greater clearness this account has from time to time separated the Spanish from the Burgundian-Hapsburg half of Charles's continental heritage, all those lands were considered by contemporaries to be one vast empire. They were brought together under Charles into as nearly unitary a political group as were many other dynastic holdings or as were the separate Spanish kingdoms themselves. That empire was generally considered as Spanish because Charles had become increasingly identified with Spain. In the case of the New World conquests and settlements however, a line of separation can be made. These new lands were obviously something outside the usual run of previous European experience. They were acquired by the novel means of discovery, although during the course of Charles's rule they were to be augmented by further exploration and by the customary European means of military conquest. Originally that portion of the Spanish Empire was looked upon as a troublesome barrier to an otherwise uninterrupted voyage to the Far East, but as the reign wore on it was found to possess value of its own.

NORTH AMERICAN EXPANSION—MAYAS AND AZTECS

The first proof of the desirability of the newly found lands came from conquests of great native kingdoms on the western continents. The initial step in the career of extending Spanish dominion to the American mainlands north of the isthmus was the occupation of Cuba. This occupation of the largest West Indian island had been entrusted to Diego Velasquez and after a rather easy series of victories over the unwarlike natives, Velasquez's forces had Cuba entirely pacified by 1514. Settlement spread rapidly; within a year several towns had sprung up, including the seat of the governor at Santiago de Cuba, and Spanish enterprise reached out to the westward. On his last voyage Columbus had touched the mainland at Honduras in September, 1502, and had met off that coast a canoe-load of Indians who wore some clothes, who had skilfully made fabrics, who carried an awning over their boat, and who gave other evidences of having reached a higher stage of culture than the naked savages of Española and the islands. But the Admiral was obsessed with the hope of finding a strait and so he bore southward without investigating the regions whence these superior natives had come.

In that vicinity, in northern Central America and southeastern Mexico, was the civilization of the Mayas. This people possessed the best and most advanced native culture of any of the Indian groups of the western hemisphere; save for vague archeological traces of problematical earlier men, the Maya people seem to have been the earliest in that region where their language has since held its own against Spanish and where the ruins of their elaborate temples still exist. To the northwest the Maya territory had been invaded by other tribes in the centuries before the appearance of Europeans, the most recent being the Toltecs and, in the 14th century, the Aztecs.

The latter people possessed an unusual genius for

war about which centered their highly organized religion and their military despotic government. They had built up an empire or confederation of subjugated tribes extending from Atlantic to Pacific and ruled this state in an orderly and effective way from their city of Tenochtitlan or modern Mexico City. This capital lay on an island in the center of Lake Texcoco, connected with shore by three great causeways; it contained stone palaces of the Aztec ruler and was inhabited by some 60,000 families. Here was the great pyramidal temple to the war-god Mexitli, from whose name the Spaniards derived the word Mexico by which we know both the city and the country. In the early 16th century the throne of the Aztec Empire was occupied by a former warrior named Montezuma who had become a priest before his elevation to the supreme power and who thus mixed with the valor of a soldier the superstition of the Aztec priestcraft. Included in the priestly lore of the Aztecs was an old prophecy that some of the gods would one day appear in human form, coming to the people of Tenochtitlan from the east, and when the Spaniards appeared in the coastal region the Emperor Montezuma was ready to believe them the supernatural beings thus foretold.

CORTÉS AND MEXICO

Once Cuba was settled and reduced to Spanish control, the governor Velasquez turned to the exploration and occupancy of the mainland which Columbus had touched. Two expeditions sent from Cuba had reached the coast of Yucatan and voyaged to the vicinity of modern Vera Cruz, when the governor entrusted to one of his companions on the Cuban invasion the command of a strong force designed to complete the work of the first expeditions. This companion was Hernando Cortés, an active, quick-witted, courageous, and determined Spaniard about thirty-three years old. Cortés possessed an unusual combination of qualities of daring, judgment, and a matchless ability to lead men. His expedition numbered somewhere around 600 men and was quite well equipped, as shown by its armament of ten brass cannon with some smaller pieces and with arquebuses (the muskets of the period) for a goodly proportion of the men, with gunpowder in sufficient quantity. Cortés also carried along sixteen horses and, since the natives had never seen a horse before, the phenomenon of a mounted man served to fill them with awe of the invaders.

On February 18, 1519, Cortés reached the island of Cozumel off Yucatan. Here he was well received by the Indians whom he converted to Christianity after delivering to them a proclamation of the majesty and might of his master King Charles and an account of the history of the Church. This became the regular procedure of notifying the Indians that they were about to enjoy the privilege of becoming Christians and subjects of the King of Castile, whether they understood what it was all about or not. It is significant that the commander took the time to spread the faith in the midst of his conquest. This invariable religious interest of the Spanish conqueror is distinctive in colonial operations and serves as a connecting link with the medieval tradition of war for the cross (and with the religious zeal of the subjects of Isabella the Catholic). At Cozumel Cortés had the good fortune to find a shipwrecked fellow-countryman who had learned the Mayan tongue, and when farther up the coast the expedition defeated a hostile chief and received from him a Mexican slave-girl who understood Mayan, Cortés had an interpreting staff capable of communicating from the Aztec language through Mayan into Spanish.

Cortés continued in steady progress up the coast to the site of Vera Cruz, converting the natives, starting trading relations, securing some gold in small quantity, and establishing the title and authority of the Castilian crown over the land. Thus he had carried out his orders and some of his followers wished to return to Cuba, but Cortés had learned of the richness and of the internal weaknesses of the Aztec Empire and he planned to press on to attempt its conquest. The calibre of the man is proved by his success in that seemingly impossible venture. He had but a handful of troops to attack a savage and warlike people with organized armies numbering tens of thousands, controlled by a centralized political power. He had to force his way through nearly three hundred miles of most difficult country, from the hot regions of the coast to the elevated plateau. He could expect no aid from Cuba for he had incurred the anger of Velasquez and had left Cuba against the opposition of the governor who tried to supplant him. But in the face of all obstacles Cortés accomplished a miracle.

First he won over the waverers in his command. Then with characteristic foresight he inquired into the political situation of the Empire he was invading and learned that many of the peoples the Aztecs had subdued were chafing under the yoke of their conquerors. Cortés accordingly played on this unrest and secured the support of some of the rebellious chieftains. He also was shrewd enough to sense the uncertainty of Montezuma whose power of decision was paralyzed by torturing doubts about the possibly divine identity of these strange white visitors so that he interposed no serious obstacle to their advance.

The story of Cortés's remarkable conquest of the Aztec state is too long to recount here, but after two years of heroic effort he overthrew the Indian power and established the authority of Charles V in Mexico in August, 1521. In the next few years the conqueror rebuilt the old Aztec capital as a Spanish city and began a vigorous organization of the territory he had won. Like his contemporaries Cortés believed in the possibility of finding a strait through the western continent to the Far East and he established settlements on the Pacific and pushed exploration rapidly. His greatest exploring triumphs lay to the southward where his lieutenants and later the conqueror in person set up colonizing centers in what are now Guatemala, Salvador and Honduras. The news of the astounding victory over the Aztec Empire and the first shipment of treasure from Mexico reached Charles V at the time he was returning to Spain for the second time, in 1522, and he rewarded Cortés with the governorship of the territory he had conquered. But Charles resembled his grandfather Ferdinand in distrusting a subject who might become too powerful and when murmurs arose against Cortés, the Emperor feared for the royal authority and quietly took the civil authority in Mexico out of the hands of Cortés. In 1528 the conqueror returned to Spain to be honored and lionized at the court, but with the loss of civil control his luck turned, his later ventures in Mexican exploration yielded nothing, and he went back again to his native land to die in 1547 in obscurity and neglect.

From the time of Cortés's conquest until the end of the reign of Charles V there followed a series of exploring and conquering ventures which opened vast stretches of the interior and the coasts of North America to geographical knowledge and enormously expanded the overseas possessions of the crown of Castile. To complete the penetration of Central America begun by Cortés, expeditions from Panama pushed northward by land and sea through Costa Rica and Nicaragua. In the latter region the tyrannical Pedrarias Davila who had executed Balboa ended his stormy career at the advanced age of ninety. Pánfilo de Narváez, in 1526, secured a grant to conquer the country from Florida northward and two years later he brought a company of 600 colonists to land near Tampa Bay. Finding the Indians hostile and hearing the usual fabulous tales of treasure just beyond, Narváez led half his force overland to the westward while the rest of the party sailed ahead in his five ships. The two groups never met and of Narváez's party only four survived and reached civilization. Narváez's treasurer, Cabeza de Vaca, and eighty men alone reached Texas after an arduous journey along the coast; the survivors melted away, all were in great distress from hunger and exhaustion, and Cabeza de Vaca was able to live because he was adopted by Indians as a medicine man and curiosity. For six years the former treasurer remained in native hands until, in 1534, he succeeded in escaping, joining three other refugees from the original party, and in toiling over the miles to Mexico, where he and his companions arrived in July, 1536. They had wandered as far west as the Pacific and Cabeza de Vaca indulged his fancy in lying stories of the riches abounding in the country he had traversed. A parallel to Narváez's venture was the expedition of Hernando de Soto, like its predecessor directed first to Florida and similarly ill-fated. De Soto, who had won distinction in Pizarro's conquest of Peru, reached Tampa Bay in 1539 and in the course of three years' wandering passed through the southern United States and discovered the Mississippi River in the waters of which he found his grave. The survivors finally built boats to carry them down the great river and succeeded in reaching the Mexican settlements on the Gulf in 1543. Meantime another exploring party under Francisco de Coronado had started from Mexico in 1540 to search for rich Indian regions to the northward. Indian rumors of vast treasure in the unexplored country, spreading among the Spaniards soon after the conquest of Mexico, had become crystallized into a story of seven native cities of unexampled wealth (called the Seven Cities of Cibola) and had received a sort of confirmation in Cabeza de Vaca's tales of having travelled through Indian lands filled with gold. The Viceroy Mendoza, who had come to Mexico as civil ruler in 1535, became convinced of the soundness of these rumors and sent Coronado with 300 Spaniards to occupy the regions. The expedition, going partly overland and partly by sea up the Gulf of California, found the fabled cities to be poverty-stricken pueblo villages and gained no treasure, but it did discover the Grand Cañon of the Colorado, did navigate to the head of the Gulf of California and up the lower course of the Colorado, and did push exploration through northern Mexico, the modern states of Arizona, New Mexico, Texas, Oklahoma, and to about the middle of

Kansas. Thus, although the immediate object of the expedition failed, Coronado had established a legal claim for the King of Castile to that huge extent of territory from Mexico up into the great central plains of the United States.

Exploration of the coast-line had likewise advanced during the same time. In 1521 a justice of the supreme court of Santo Domingo named Ayllon sent a caravel under Francisco de Gordillo to explore the mainland. Gordillo coasted to about the site of Georgetown Entrance in South Carolina (latitude 33° 30′ N.) where he loaded his ship with Indians and returned. The Indians were liberated at Santo Domingo by Ayllon and Gordillo was condemned for attempting slave-hunting. Ayllon in 1526 conducted a colonizing party farther up the Atlantic coast and made two efforts to settle, the second being somewhere between the site of Jamestown, Virginia, and the Cape Fear River, but fever and Indian attacks decimated the party and the settlements were abandoned. At about the same time another voyage linked the section of the coast which Ayllon visited with the vicinity of Newfoundland. A Portuguese captain named Estevan Gómez who had deserted the command of Magellan on the voyage of circumnavigation, received a commission from Charles to explore the Atlantic coast of the New World in search of a strait to the Spice Islands and sailed from Spain in 1525. Gómez struck the coast between Newfoundland and Maine and sailed southward to the fortieth parallel, giving Charles a claim by discovery to the entire eastern seaboard of the United States. On the Pacific side of the continent Cortés had carried out seaward explorations, sending ships up the coast of Lower California to the latitude of 28° or 29°. In

1542-43 a small squadron skirted the coast of California (under command of Cabrillo who died on the way, and then of the pilot Ferrelo) as far as Cape Mendocino which was named in honor of the Viceroy Mendoza.

THE INCAS

Although the year 1543 saw Spanish activity complete the exploration and conquest, and progress with the occupation, of a territory in North America many times the size of the empire of Charles V in Europe, similar triumphs in South America meanwhile increased the extent of the Emperor's colonial holdings. The great conquest to parallel that of Cortés was the victory of Francisco Pizarro over the powerful native state of the Incas. Like the Aztecs the Inca rulers of Peru headed an Indian state of remarkable political attainments and organization. The culture of this people exhibited a combination of barbarity and advancement similar to that of the Aztecs. The Incas were inferior to their Mexican contemporaries in development of writing and astronomy and calendars, but surpassed the Aztecs in agriculture, in the use of domesticated animals, in road-building, and in their freedom from blood-thirsty and cannibalistic religious practices. Their religion was Sun worship and served to strengthen the political authority of the absolute ruler, the Inca, who was believed to be directly descended from the Sun.

At Cuzco the Incas had their capital. In this city and others in the Inca Empire were to be found buildings of massive blocks of stone, so well built that notwithstanding the fact that no cement was used in their construction they have withstood earthquakes for centuries. Not long before the 16th century the Incas had been extending their sway over other native peoples whom they appear to have treated with something of the wise humanity of the Romans in dealing with their conquered populations. The Inca Empire embraced the territory of the modern states of Ecuador, Peru, Bolivia, northern Chile and the northwestern corner of Argentina. Reminiscent of the situation among the Aztecs there existed dissension among the Incas on the eve of the invasion of a Spanish force. The last Inca had divided his Empire between two of his sons and one, Atahualpa by name, had overthrown his half-brother and reunited the state, leaving embers of dissatisfaction and revolt among some of his subjects.

PIZARRO'S CONQUEST

Francisco Pizarro, the hero of this conquest, was inferior to Cortés on most counts of character and ability, and the equal of Cortés only in daring. Sprung from the gutter, with no resources but his wits and his sword, Pizarro had knocked about Darien for some years when he gained an opportunity to head an exploring expedition from Panama in 1524. On this venture and a subsequent journey he went southward to the outskirts of the Inca Empire and saw evidences of the high civilization of the natives and of gold work and precious stones which gave promise of rich spoil. But Pizarro and the two adventurers as poor as himself, with whom he had entered into partnership before his first commission, could not possibly raise the funds to equip a strong enough force to cope with the military power of the Inca. Accordingly Pizarro went to Spain to lay the project before the Emperor and to secure aid from him. When the adventurer reached Charles's court in 1528 Cortés was there and it has been conjectured that the successful conqueror of Mexico may have given Pizarro suggestions which he later put into use in attacking the Inca state.

After some delay Pizarro received a royal grant, or *capitulación,* and returned in 1530 with some recruits from Spain and with the royal authority for raising a conquering force. By this time however the early fever of enthusiasm for adventure had largely disappeared in the Indies; bitter experience had taught the men on the spot that privation and hardship were far more frequently the lot of explorers than jewels and treasure. It was by dint of much effort that Pizarro and his partners raised a company of under two hundred men. At the head of this force Pizarro sailed from Panama early in 1531 while his associate Diego Almagro was to follow later with reinforcements and additional supplies. There ensued another miraculous achievement; like Cortés, Pizarro accomplished the seemingly impossible feat of invading the Inca Empire, seizing the native Emperor, traversing the garrisoned country across the high ridges of the Andes to occupy Cuzco, and sweeping away the Inca state. On November 15, 1533, Pizarro entered the capital city and although neither natives nor Spaniards entirely realized it at the moment, the conquest was a fact and the Empire of the Incas another realm of the Castilian monarch Charles V. Unlike the conquest of Cortés this Peruvian conquest was to suffer from internecine disorders; civil wars between the conquerors and rebellions against royal officials sent out from Spain, raged intermittently until 1550. During the progress of the invasion unprecedented quantities of treasure had fallen into the conquerors' hands, the Inca Atahualpa had paid a ransom of a roomful of gold and the Peruvian habit of covering the roofs and walls of their temples with plates of the precious metal had yielded rich booty. The mines of Peru were valuable and though the frequent internal wars interrupted the output, a fairly steady stream of bullion passed into the royal coffers during the late forties and early fifties of the century.

CHILE, THE AMAZON, NEW GRANADA, THE PLATA

While civil wars ran on in Peru, other parts of the South American continent were opened up by the efforts of explorers and conquerors. The first attempt to occupy the region of Chile by Almagro, Pizarro's partner and later enemy in the civil wars, brought no rewarding find of treasure and was abandoned. The nitrate deserts south of Lake Titicaca which are today so valuable were then forbidding wastes and so serious an obstacle to settlement that it was not until 1540 that a Castilian veteran, Pedro de Valdivia, led a party into that country. With the invaluable assistance of his lieutenant Francisco de Aguirre who was a born organizer, Valdivia founded the present capital of Chile and other towns, fought the warlike Araucanian Indians to the south (an unconquerable and conspicuously independent people) and laid the foundations for orderly and permanent colonial settlement. To the northward of Cuzco the conquerors occupied the region of modern Ecuador early in the day and from there made important advances north and eastward. To the east of Quito it was rumored that cinnamon trees grew and a younger brother of the Conqueror, Gonzalo Pizarro, in 1540 led an expedition across the Andes in

search of it. He found some of the spice but suffered
such disastrous hardships that he had to neglect everything else in the effort to keep his men alive. Gonzalo
Pizarro in desperate straits for food contrived to build
a boat and sent one of his subordinates, Francisco de
Orellana, down the Napo River to look for supplies.
Orellana deserted his commander and floated for
months down a mighty river to the sea, finally making
his way up the eastern coast to the Caribbean settlements and bestowing the name of Amazon on the
stream he had discovered. Gonzalo Pizarro by heroic
effort fought his way back to Quito with a handful of
men.

North of Quito on the high plateau of Cundina-
marca was the home of the Chibcha Indians who had
attained a relatively high stage of culture, comparable
in many ways to that of Aztec and Inca. In 1536 a
lawyer, Gonzalo Ximenez de Quesada, who had come
to the region about Santa Marta on the northern coast
of South America as chief judge of the colony there,
led an expedition up the valley of the Magdalena River
into the country of the Chibchas. Quesada conquered
the natives of the plateau, founded the city of Santa
Fé de Bogotá, and christened the region New Granada.
On the heels of his conquest two rival explorers arrived
on the scene, one of them reaching the plateau from the
south in the process of expanding northward from
Quito.

The rest of the northern seaboard of the continent had been the field of various activities from
early in the period of discovery. Opening on the Caribbean as it does, that strip of coast partook of the development of the islands and had been used as a center
of pearl-fishing and slave-hunting, with such cruel mis-

treatment of the natives that orderly and peaceful occupation was long delayed. As a result of the early efforts to exploit and to settle that region along with the West Indies it became known, in distinction to the islands, as *Tierra Firme,* or the "mainland," and from that Spanish name came the term "Spanish Main" which we vaguely associate with piracy in the tropics in general, but which means only the coast of modern Venezuela and Guiana.

One more portion of South America was incorporated into the colonial empire of Charles V, the region of La Plata. Unlike the other territorial gains in the New World during the Emperor's reign, this area was developed directly from Spain and not by expeditions based on centers in the western hemisphere. Because it faced the open Atlantic and was cut off from the other South American settlements, it was exploited directly. In 1526 Sebastian Cabot was sent out by Charles and a group of merchants of Seville to find a strait to the Spice Islands. Cabot sailed up the Plata estuary some distance and founded a short-lived settlement. He proved that the strait did not lie in that great river system, but in 1533 the notion that the Plata might provide a more direct route to Peru revived interest in the region and Pedro de Mendoza came out to settle there. His first foundation on the site of modern Buenos Aires was forced to move up the river to Asunción in 1537, a city which has survived and is the present capital of Paraguay. Later the veteran explorer Cabeza de Vaca was sent out by the royal government to head the colony and to investigate the possibility of an overland road to Peru. The latter project produced nothing feasible because of the difficulty of the terrain but the settlements in the Plata valley continued.

MAGELLAN AND THE PHILIPPINES

The final increment of colonial territory which Charles's reign brought into the Castilian orbit was the Philippine archipelago. This one holding in the Far East, the quarter of the earth which had been the lodestar for all the voyages of discovery, came into Spanish possession as a result of the epoch-making expedition of Ferdinand Magellan. Magellan's voyage was one of the early ventures of Charles as a Spanish sovereign. He had commissioned the effort in 1519 and the triumphant return of one ship of Magellan's fleet had occurred in 1522, the year of the Emperor's return to Spain. Magellan had clearly established a claim to the archipelago by priority of occupation; more than that, Charles was eager to utilize the voyage to gain possession of the spice-bearing Moluccas and at the time it was difficult to say whether these islands lay on Portugal's or Castile's side of the line fixed by the Treaty of Tordesillas. The Portuguese were alert to maintain their monopoly of the spice trade and contested vigorously the claim of the Emperor. A joint Spanish-Portuguese commission (the Junta of Badajoz) tried to determine the question of the Tordesillas line and to adjust the claims amicably, but was unable to reach an agreement. Charles meanwhile sent several expeditions to clinch his hold on some of the Moluccas. They failed to secure a firm hold in that island group, and Charles in 1529 made a treaty with the King of Portugal renouncing claims to them and fixing an eastern demarcation line. The

Philippines, however, were not claimed by the Portuguese and Charles considered them his territory although on Portugal's side of the line. In 1542 his Viceroy in Mexico sent six ships under the command of Villalobos from Navidad on the west coast of Mexico to the archipelago. Villalobos cruised about the group, discovering many new islands, fixing more firmly the title of the Emperor to the group, and, as his most lasting accomplishment, bestowed on the archipelago the name it has borne ever since. Magellan had named the isles for Saint Lazarus but Villalobos christened them for Charles's son Philip, "the Philippines, after our most fortunate Prince." Their productive use was to come in the next reign.

COLONIAL SUMMARY

On the whole the reign of Charles marks an age of conquest and organization of the huge empire across the oceans. When he came to the thrones of the Catholic Kings, the period of discovery had yielded only the barest beginning of mainland settlement in the Americas and the island colonies of the West Indies were in a weak condition economically. In the islands the decay of the native population and the consequent shortage of labor had rendered them unproductive and of decreasing value. By the end of the reign of Charles the incredible territorial addition extending from the straits of Magellan to central Mexico had been made on the continents and strong legal claims had been established still farther northward. This meant practically the full extent of Spanish colonial limits in the western hemisphere (save for Louisiana and California). At his accession the revenue coming to the crown from the colonies was insignificant; at his abdication Charles was receiving undreamed-of wealth from the gold and silver mines of Mexico and Peru. During the Emperor's reign, moreover, the fundamentals of the colonial organization were established, the machinery created for governing the Indies both at home and overseas, and the position of civil and ecclesiastical authority defined.

SEA-POWER

In another direction this period of imperial expansion of the Spains is strikingly significant, namely in the consideration of sea-power and in the relation of maritime strength to the world's history. The term sea-power in this discussion means something more than naval might; rather, the term includes the combined factors of geographical situation, economic activity, national vigor, and possession of trading posts or colonies which permit the secure conduct of sea-borne commerce upon the great ocean highways of the globe. The military element, although not the sole component, is an important one because fighting force has been essential to protect merchant shipping and to secure command of the water for territorial extension or political advantage. At just the time the Iberian states were expanding into great oversea empires, sea-power was becoming wider than ever before; from the old center, the Mediterranean, and from the Baltic and European coastal waters, the era of discovery had brought the oceans themselves to the fore as the critical area for the action of sea-power. The Mediterranean Sea, which had been the vital naval arena since classic antiquity, was still an important route of commerce as evidenced by the considerable maritime strength of

Venice and Genoa and by the duels for control between Spain and the Turks, but in the reign of Charles the oceans became paramount in importance. Hence the geographical position of the Iberian peninsula with extensive coast-lines on both waters made Spain and Portugal early leaders in sea-power. Spain in particular was the outstanding transitional region between Mediterranean and Atlantic, she was the logical power to hold colonies in the western hemisphere, and since she was so intimately bound up with political and commercial developments in both the Old and New Worlds while Charles V wore the Spanish crowns, it was obvious that Spain must be strong in eastern and western waters alike. Moreover, since her seaboard ran with those of the maritime trading powers of the future (France, England and Charles's native Low Countries, later the independent United Netherlands), and since the Emperor's continental policies involved rivalry with the Valois, Spain was forced to defend her interests on the water. Because of their political history prior to the 16th century, she and Portugal were fitted to take the lead in empire-building as in exploration. They expanded into the Orient and the Americas, they prospered from production of precious metals and from the spice trade; that expansion and influx of wealth were possible because Portugal and Spain were in every sense of the word great Sea Powers. Able to dominate the ocean routes from Europe to their imperial possessions and strong enough navally to control the waters around their colonies, they could and did maintain strict monopolies of the trade and development of their empires during the first half of the 16th century. The force of this maritime factor was to be brought out in the latter half of the century when the Iberian sea predominance was no longer unchallenged and complete.[1]

ABDICATION

For all the unprecedented magnitude of his empire in both hemispheres, Charles V had known rather the cares of high place and its responsibilities than any joy in power. He had borne heavy burdens without relief or cessation, he had journeyed up and down Europe repeatedly, he had found his political activity complicated by the necessity of dealing with a score of pressing problems at the same time, and he had for years suffered from digestive troubles which in his later years had become acute torture. Not even the revenues of Spain had sufficed to meet the constant expense of such extensive political operations as his, and his worries had through all the reign been increased by the pinch of poverty. Because Charles had not shirked his duties but had exerted himself to the limit of his energy, he was prematurely worn out and aged by the end of his conflict with the Lutherans. Consequently, in 1554, Charles determined on the unusual step of abdicating from his high position, of turning his Spanish possessions over to his son (and in the case of the German lands, to his brother), and of ending his days in retirement as a private individual. On January 16, 1556, after having previously bestowed his Burgundian lands upon his son Philip, Charles formally made over to his heir all the Spanish dominions in the Old and

[1] It is interesting to observe that the relation between sea-power and the fortunes of nations was not fully realized until the later 19th century when a Captain of the United States Navy, Alfred T. Mahan, wrote the first of several studies of sea-power.

the New Worlds. To the Spains the eventful reign of their first Hapsburg King had brought an increase of lands and greatness beyond the wildest dream of romance or fancy. Yet that expansion to imperial greatness and that rise to political domination in the old field of European politics came at high cost to the Iberian realms. For they were suddenly jerked up to that pinnacle without time to build the necessary foundation and without having developed the resources to support so vast an undertaking as the maintenance of the Spanish Empire Charles had established. Finally, there is to be noted in addition to the internal factors just mentioned, the fear and the hostility of rival states which felt their safety threatened by the might of the Spains of Charles V.

CHAPTER III

PHILIP II—THE EMPIRE, THE FAITH, AND SEA-POWER

PHILIP II—HIS INHERITANCE AND HIS CHARACTER

To any well-informed observer of European politics in 1556 it must have seemed that the mighty Spanish Hapsburg power of Philip II was a thing of permanence and unshakeable solidity. The new King of the Spains, the master of the lion's share of the far-flung imperial possessions of Charles V, headed an imposing array of dynastic lands. It is true that the events of the closing years of his father's reign, particularly the failure of the Emperor's policy in Germany, had necessitated the division of the holdings Charles had possessed in the east. Charles V had been unable to secure support from the territorial princes of the Holy Roman Empire for Philip as imperial heir-apparent, and had been compelled to pass the inheritance of the Hapsburg lands to Ferdinand, his brother and regent in the Empire. For all his Hapsburg ancestry, Philip showed the effects of the Hispanicization his father had undergone and was as Spanish as a Castilian grandee. To this circumstance of his appearing an alien to the Germans, arose their opposition to him, a curious reversal of the situation prevailing in Spain on Charles's succession to the Catholic Kings and a parallel to it as well.

Yet although Charles had been forced to split his vast dominions in Europe, he had bequeathed no inconsiderable heritage to his beloved Spanish son. Partly to compensate Philip for the loss of the Empire and the Austrian patrimony of his house, and partly to continue the strategical concentration against the dynastic enemy France, the Emperor gave to Philip the old Burgundian domains of the Low Countries, Luxemburg and Franche Comté, and the duchy of Milan, which Charles had gained outright during his reign. These territories had never before had any Spanish connection and they were now united directly with the lands of the Catholic Kings: the realms of the Spains, the Italian kingdoms of Naples and Sicily, Cerdagne and Roussillon, and the *presidios* in North Africa. Moreover, as King of Castile, Philip II inherited the great colonial empire of the Indies. From his New World possessions there was coming a stream of treasure, the yield of the mines of Mexico and Peru, substantial in actual quantity and magnified far beyond its real amount by the common report of envious and alarmed European rivals. With that vast political and economic heritage, what could be more natural than to suppose that the new King of the Spains would increase his power and prestige as had his father in the preceding reign, and that he would create an even greater and more menacing predominance over Europe?

International rivalries of the period of Charles V had been dynastic in character; the Council of Trent and the Counter-Reformation (or Catholic-Reformation) brought the religious element more strongly to the fore, and by a close union of religion and politics transformed European affairs. At the same time colonial and economic factors, growing out of the overseas

expansion of Portugal and Castile, became decisively
active in the international situation. Because of the
developments of his father's reign, Philip II was heavily involved in the international conflict dynastically
and imperially, and because of his intensely religious
temperament he was deeply drawn into the world-wide
struggle as champion of the old faith and church.

In the mid-sixteenth century the personal qualities
of monarchs counted heavily in the history of the
world; the national states centered about their absolute sovereigns with a completeness unknown to the
earlier feudally limited kings or to the later rulers
bound by powerful nobility or powerful parliament. A
striking example of the influence of the character of a
king upon the fortunes of his country is furnished by
the Spanish Empire under Philip II. It is not easy
for people of the English-speaking tradition to form an
accurate opinion of Philip; it requires an effort to re-
move from our minds the inherited prejudice of hostile
national and Protestant propaganda spread during the
long struggle of England and of the Lutherans and Cal-
vinists against the Spanish ruler four centuries and a
half ago. As we discard the partisan conception of
Philip we throw out the belief that he was a monster
of cruelty or a malevolent hobgoblin and we are able
to understand why his subjects and their descendants
gave him the admiring title of "El Rey Prudente," the
Prudent King. His character shows as a dominating
trait an unswerving and very high sense of duty. This
made him toil unsparingly to serve the state he controlled and to carry forward the cause of God on earth
as it seemed so plainly manifested to him. Without
conspicuous brilliance he nevertheless possessed a
shrewd mind, capacity for concentration and hard

work, and a tenacity and conscientiousness far above
the average. Modest, cautious, patient, simple and un-
ostentatious in his living, gentle with his intimates and
loved by them, devoted to Spain and ceaseless in his
endeavors to promote Spanish interests, he was per-
fectly suited to make a successful local ruler and to
complete the internal unification of Iberia. But the
circumstances of his birth and of his time forced Philip
to be a prominent actor on a wider stage than the
peninsula and his own nature and his inheritance made
his conduct of larger affairs decisive for the future and
disastrous to the Spanish Empire.

It was the element of religion, strengthened by the
religious training and conceptions of Philip, which
proved of so great consequence in world history. Both
his parents were grandchildren of Isabella the Catholic
and much of the intense religious fervor of the ardent
queen came down to Philip. As a boy he pictured his
father constantly warring against heretic and infidel;
he was brought up to join his mother and the ladies of
the court in hour-long prayers for the success of the
Emperor's battles for the faith. He was, moreover, a
thorough-going Spaniard, so that it was natural for him
to hate deviation from the old church. With the family and national influences surrounding him, Philip
came naturally by his firm belief that he was a divinely
chosen instrument to lead Europe back to religious
unity. This belief in his mission led him to follow the
way which his inherited conviction taught him to be
the path God must desire. It sustained him in un-
shaken confidence through the reverses and failures of
the last years of his reign. Charles V aimed at establishing the religious unification of Christendom under
his political supremacy and his son accepted that aim

as the great object of his life, the very reason for his existence. Peoples, kings, and popes were in his sight accessories to be used by the Spanish Cæsar in his divine mission. Consequently Philip's piety, deep and genuine as it was, was unique in its independence of the ecclesiastical authority; even the Church as an institution and all its officers seemed to him instruments for his wielding in the heavenly cause. He opposed the papal authority and he manipulated secular politics like the most cynical of Renaissance statesmen, yet in everything he was motivated by the fixed idea that he was acting solely for the faith. For the same end Philip freely poured out Spanish treasure and military strength, continued to drain Spain and the Indies of money, and like his father kept up the exhaustion of the economic capabilities of his Empire. Yet for all their distress the Spaniards, in whom the crafty policy of Ferdinand and Isabella had inspired a mighty religious exaltation, gladly bore the burdens of supporting their king's championship of Roman Christianity in its royal Spanish form. National pride also prompted Philip's subjects to aid his projects. Unlike his father who was immersed in cosmopolitan activities, Philip directed his widespread affairs from Iberia and made Spain the center and source of his policies.

RELATIONS WITH FRANCE

At the time Charles V abdicated the Iberian crowns, Philip II found himself with a general European war on his hands. This was the fifth Hapsburg-Valois war, produced by the usual clash of interests between Henry II of France and the Emperor and by the violent hatred of the Hapsburgs entertained by Pope Paul IV, a member of the Neapolitan family of Caraffa who had long opposed Spanish ascendancy in Italy. In 1559 an end came to the war in the Peace of Cateau-Cambrésis. This treaty was another epoch-making settlement. Territorially it returned captured places which each power had taken, with the important exception of the famous three Bishoprics of Metz, Toul, and Verdun on the eastern bounds of France which have been important positions in European history from that day to this and which were left to France by the treaty. France was also to retain possession of Calais, the last English foothold on the continent and the last remnant of the Angevin lands of the middle ages. The peace was designed to enable Philip and Henry II to coöperate in repressing Protestantism and the friendship between the two countries was sealed by the marriage of the French princess Elizabeth de Valois to the Spanish King as his third wife. For Spain the treaty promised to end the French practice of aiding Protestants in Hapsburg dominions and it cleared the way for Philip to devote his strength to the cause of the faith. For France the treaty marked the redirection of French policy toward the north and east, toward the desired realization of the "natural frontiers," and away from Italy where for over sixty years French kings had dissipated their resources in chimerical ventures.

Amidst universal rejoicing in France over Cateau-Cambrésis, Henry II was accidentally killed in a tournament celebrating the treaty; in the removal of that strong monarch Philip found an opportunity to advance his inspired cause and the interests of Spain. In succession to Henry three of his sons reigned, but since they were weak and incompetent the actual power lay in the hands of Henry's widow, Catherine de'

Medici, a stout, goggle-eyed daughter of the great
Florentine house. Many difficulties beset Catherine,
the jealous opposition of the strong border family of
the Guise from Lorraine, the turbulence of the other
nobles which found an outlet in the devastating civil
and religious wars from 1561 to 1593, and the question of the treatment of Huguenots. Philip took advantage of the weakness of Catherine's position to
press on his mother-in-law a vigorous policy against
the Protestants in France, but although a Catholic, the
queen-mother was essentially interested in keeping the
crown for her sons and in gaining political strength
rather than in forcing religious uniformity upon
France.

At the outset Catherine de' Medici had to
defer to Philip because she needed his support; the
massacre of Protestants on St. Bartholomew's Eve
(1572) took place with royal connivance. Later she
encouraged French Huguenots to encroach upon the
Spanish Empire in Florida and in Brazil, gave aid to
Philip's rebellious Dutch subjects, and provided a fleet
for the Portuguese pretender.[1] Disappointed in his
hopes of exerting a controlling influence in the French
kingdom, Philip was able to retaliate by aiding heavily
the Catholic League formed by the Duke of Guise in
1576. This organization of the Catholic extremists opposed the Huguenots at the other end of the religious
scale and the larger party of moderates between the
two extremes. In the war of factions resulting in
France, a nationalist issue cut across the religious, for
the extreme parties were calling on foreigners for help,
the League on Catholic Spain and the Huguenots on
Protestant England. The friend of the ultra-Catholic

[1] See below, pp. 127-129.

faction was the old national enemy Spain, considered with good reason the chief menace to France. It was this element of nationalism which gave the contemptible Henry III a following and made the middle party formidable. When in 1588 Henry III had his rival the Duke of Guise assassinated, only to fall himself a victim to the dagger the following year, the last Valois in the direct line was dead and Philip came forward as a candidate for the French throne in the right of his deceased wife, Elizabeth de Valois, or of their daughter the Infanta Isabella. Against him was the claim of the head of the Protestant party, Henry of Navarre, as a collateral relative of the Valois kings. For Philip the situation in France was of the gravest importance; the political desirability of expanding Spanish control across the Pyrenees is obvious and to his religious ardor it was unbearable that a heretic should wear the French crown. Four years of warfare saw the national principle ascendant over the religious in the minds of Frenchmen and saw general defeats for the forces of the Prudent King in the field. Finally, in 1593, Henry of Navarre, now Henry IV of France, accepted the Catholic faith with the cynical comment, "Paris is worth a mass," thus gaining the recognition of all his subjects. When five years later Henry issued the Edict of Nantes giving toleration to Protestants in France, Philip's ambitions and policy in France culminated in total defeat. At the end of Philip's reign all possibility of Spanish ascendancy over France had gone and with the extension of tolerance to Huguenots failure had come to the dearest aim of the King of the Spains.

REVOLT OF THE NETHERLANDS

Another serious problem on the continent was the revolt in the Netherlands which broke out about ten years after Charles V had turned over those provinces to his son. The rising in the Low Countries was international in its implications, involving France and England and giving them an opportunity to play off their hostility to Philip by aiding the Dutch rebels. France was concerned because of the proximity of the provinces, because the Protestant Netherlanders in the north were Calvinist in doctrine and so in close touch with French Huguenots, and because it was an effective way for the Valois to strike back at Philip's interference in France by covertly helping the Dutch. For England there were many reasons for interest in the struggle. There had been since the middle ages a close economic connection between wool-growing England and the wool-manufacturing towns of the Low Countries. There was the factor increasingly appreciated by the government of Elizabeth, that the safety of England depends on the country across the narrow seas being held by a friendly or a weak power. This conception of the Netherlands as Britain's first line of defence was clearly marked as soon as the ruler of the Spanish Empire, to which the Burgundian lands belonged, entertained designs on the island.[1] It was

[1] In the years to come the same principle was to bring England into continental wars to defend British interests by defending the Low Countries against the aggression of a strong power. Instances of this occurred during the wars of Louis XIV of France, during the Napoleonic wars and in 1914 at the outbreak of the World War when Germany invaded Belgium. Credit for the appreciation of this necessity for England and for its erection into a conscious maxim of British statecraft is usually given to Elizabeth's minister William Cecil, Lord Burghley.

conversely the importance of the geographical relationship which had caused Charles to plan the marriage of his cousin Mary Tudor to Philip II (concluded in 1554). For the Emperor, in his desire to bestow the Low Countries upon his son, hoped to secure the flank of the long line of sea-communication to Spain by renewed alliance with England, and Charles realized how difficult Philip's control of the Netherlands would be without the friendship of the island kingdom. But the fear of foreign domination caused Mary's councillors to draft the marriage settlement in such a way that Philip possessed no hold on England when Mary died childless in 1558.

From the standpoint of Spain's interests the Emperor's bequest of his Burgundian lands to Philip's Spanish Empire seemed contemporaneously advantageous, but from our distance in time, and to our after-the-fact perspective, it was unfortunate. Spain had paid heavily for the magnitude of Charles's burdens; the splitting of the Hapsburg dominions in Europe bade fair to relieve Spain of the crushing weight of impoverishing responsibilities beyond her strength to support. The same costly burden, however, was perpetuated in linking the Netherlands up to the rest of Philip's lands. The Low Countries had never had customs, traditions or political experience in common with Iberia. They regarded Charles as one of themselves since he had been born in Ghent and reared among the Flemings, but his son was completely an alien. The wealthy and self-sufficient cities with their independent and autonomy-loving burghers hated such Spanish things as the Inquisition and autocratic government, and they feared that Philip would force a foreign, centralized system upon them. Consequently the Low Countries were certain to revolt against the rigid religious and political domination of Philip.

In 1565 the King's efforts to stamp out the Calvinist heresy which had spread into the southern Burgundian towns from the neighboring industrial towns of France precipitated a general resistance which was national rather than religious, as is indicated by the appearance of Catholics as well as Protestants in opposition to the Spanish Inquisition and to Spanish absolutism. The leader of the rebellion, William the Silent, Prince of Orange, was one of many Catholic nobles who came into the struggle to resist Philip's encroachments on the old cherished institutions of the provinces. The rebellion continued throughout the remaining forty-three years of Philip's reign, always a heavy drain on Spain's resources and a liability in international politics for the Spanish Empire. Under the successive governorships of Philip's sister Margaret of Parma, of the Duke of Alva, of Luis de Requesens, of Don John of Austria, and of Alexander of Parma, every shade of treatment from repressive frightfulness to attempted leniency failed to end the revolt or to produce a general *modus vivendi*. The utmost Philip was able to salvage from the turmoil and bitterness of the rebellion was a separation of the ten southern provinces, predominantly Catholic in religion, from the seven northern Protestant provinces; the Catholic districts remained under Spanish control while the northern group, the United Provinces, became the Dutch Republic, whose legal independence was recognized in the Peace of Westphalia in 1648. From this religious separation of the Low Countries has come the present division between the states of Belgium (Catholic) and Holland (Protestant). So violent and lengthy a struggle demanded of

Spain tremendous effort and sacrifice, a ruinous drain
in a cause destined to fail and for an object widely removed from the welfare of the Spanish Empire.

THE INFIDEL—MEDITERRANEAN NAVAL POWER

Among the problems in foreign affairs handed on
from Charles V, Philip found the war against the infidel a constant and troublesome concern. Even though
the Prudent King did not have to defend the Danube
valley directly, he encountered many of the difficulties
of the late Emperor in repelling corsair and Turk in
the Mediterranean. To Philip with his zeal for Christianity this was a welcome sphere of activity and even
a lukewarm churchman would have been stirred by the
audacity of the Moslem piratical attacks on Spanish
shipping and coasts. But it was true of the Prudent
King as it had been of his father before him, that
money and freedom from other political cares were
lacking and only rarely could he devote full strength
and all his attention to the war on Islam. Although
the Spanish viceroys in Naples and Sicily had permanent galley squadrons to defend the Italian shores of
the Empire, Philip practised the economy of relying on
the Knights of Saint John at Malta to do most of the
fighting against the Ottoman fleet and the North African corsairs. The Moslems possessed a worthy successor to Kheir-ed-Din (Barbarossa) in the bold and
skillful Dragut who harried the Christians of the Mediterranean until he fell in 1565. The old Franco-Turkish alliance languished after the death of Henry II and
during the internal disorders of the civil and religious
wars in France, but the Ottoman fleet cruised to the
westward often and the Barbary pirates were always

active. The result was that every summer witnessed
naval activity. In 1560 Philip participated with the
Knights in an operation in force against Dragut's
stronghold at Tripoli which began by taking the island
of Gerba but ended as a costly defeat. Five years later
a long-expected concentration of Turkish and corsair
power against Malta nearly wiped out that valuable
outpost of Christendom. When the Turks began the
celebrated siege of the island Philip moved so slowly
to the relief that no credit for the repulse of Islam belongs to him; the tenacity and heroism of the defend-
ers and the energy of the Spanish commanders in Italy
turned back the attack with heavy loss. The treacherous seizure of the island of Cyprus from Venice by the
Turks in 1570 awoke the west once more to the Moslem menace and the efforts of Pope Pius V succeeded
in creating another Holy League, one of the few genuine holy leagues of the many bearing that name during
the 16th century. Made up of the Pope, Spain, Venice, the Knights at Malta and some of the Italian maritime cities, notably Genoa, Philip made the largest
contribution to the force of the League and his illegitimate half-brother Don John of Austria headed the
Christian armada. A great naval concentration, after
the usual delays, sought out the Ottoman fleet and won
a resounding victory off Lepanto at the mouth of the
Gulf of Corinth on October 7, 1571. So great was the
renown of this victory that all Europe rejoiced at the
notion that the might of Islam on the water had at last
been broken and the belief has persisted to our time
that Lepanto broke the Turkish naval power for good
and all. That is too sweeping a verdict; the fleet of
the League followed precedent by separating after the
victory, failed to follow it up by pursuing the fugitive

galleys or striking more mortal blows at Ottoman ports, and did not free the seas from Moslem piratical activity. It did achieve a partial success, it restored Christian morale and confidence, it redounded hugely to the credit of Spain, but it was the line of weak Sultans and the growing decadence of Ottoman administration which weakened the Turkish navy rather than the battle. Amid the universal acclaim in Europe, Lepanto raised the maritime prestige of Philip's Empire and made Spain the pre-eminent naval power of the Mediterranean.

Apart from operations in the open sea, Spain had since the time of the Catholic Kings been interested in possessions along the North African coast. The reign of Charles V had seen a loss of influence in that region, yet Philip inherited some *presidios,* alliances of varying effectiveness with native rulers, and in particular a protectorate over the kingdom of Tunis. Yet in spite of the triumph at Lepanto, Spanish influence declined in Barbary. In 1574 the Turks regained Tunis and in the later years of the reign the Prudent King's hold on the *presidios* weakened. During the succeeding reigns Spain's control declined until Oran, the last of the *presidios,* fell into Moslem hands in 1791. The tradition of holding territory in North Africa was so strong that the Spanish people in 1907 welcomed the acquisition of the present Spanish zone of Morocco.

INTERNAL AFFAIRS

Internally the Iberian kingdoms which formed the nucleus of the Spanish Empire were in a better position to draw closer together in a national union than at any time since the days of Rome. Philip II could start

where his father left off in the task of uniting the
Spains and Philip possessed the great advantage of
being a Spaniard born, one with his subjects in sym-
pathy and national feeling, loved as a native where
Charles had met the traditional distrust of the foreigner. As a boy Philip had shown gravity and seri-
ousness beyond his years and the Emperor began his
son's political instruction very early, emphasizing the
importance of retaining authority in the ruler's hands,
of keeping his own council, of distrusting men and
thus avoiding the possibility that any one adviser become indispensable or too powerful. All these warn-
ings were designed to maintain the king's absolutism;
in long letters and in a political testament to his heir
Charles reiterated this advice. Philip learned his lesson well. He carried on the principles of autocracy
of his predecessor and to that end he kept all details
of government in his grasp, insisting on handling all
matters in person and reading all documents without
ever learning what minutiæ to delegate to subordinates.
For that reason partly, and partly because Philip believed that in his divine mission he could wait indefi-
nitely for God to bring to pass the things Philip was
planning, the business of administering the great Empire suffered wearisome delay. Laborious, patient and
watchful, the King toiled through all the business of
state, procrastinating in policy and in action, since the
instrument of Providence could afford to wait. Thus
he earned for Spain the reputation for proverbial slow-
ness and contemporaries spoke of Philip's "leaden foot"
(*pié plombo*). In that cautious patience Philip stopped
short of ending the old de-centralization of royal control; like his ancestors he strengthened despotism but
he did not abolish completely the separate existence of

the old kingdoms. In the last decade of the century and of his reign Philip suppressed the ancient traditional "Liberties" of Aragon. Yet Philip, though curbing the Aragonese power of limitation on royal authority, did not wipe out the lines of separate existence and merge the eastern realms with Castile. He and his successors were still Kings of the Spains and not strictly Kings of Spain.

The machinery of government under the Prudent King centered about the Councils and reduced the Cortes to further impotence. As the most convenient mechanism for absolutism the Councils reached their furthest extension and importance in this reign. Philip added a Council of Flanders, a Council of Italy, and, after 1580, a Council of Portugal; in each body Castilians made up the membership and natives of the regions concerned had no part. The Cortes of Castile continued to meet but it was a weak body, subservient to the monarch, obediently voting taxes and grants upon request, and reduced to the representatives of the eighteen cities of Castile with no members of the nobility or clergy attending. On the legal side Philip started the recodification of the law, the *Nueva Recopilación,* which followed the old line of descent from Roman Law and which threw the emphasis rather on Castilian procedure and Castilian institutions than on Aragonese. In domestic affairs Philip tended toward a general Castilianization, reflecting in the westward shifting of Spanish things the growing importance of the American side of the Empire, at the expense of the older Mediterranean portion of imperial Aragon.

Economically the reign was ruinous to Spain. Philip inherited an impossible situation. An empty treasury, stifling taxation, and loans from German and Italian

bankers which had mortgaged Spanish income for
years ahead, bore witness to the financial necessities
of Charles V. The loans absorbed the royal share of
the bullion pouring in from the Indies, and, as soon as
past debts might be cleared, there were the obligations
Philip had contracted to raise money for his wide operations in behalf of the faith. Most of the land of Spain
was owned by the nobles and church corporations who
paid intermittent contributions under royal pressure instead of regular taxes. The tax system was unwise in
that it struck at the sources of prosperity rather than
drawing upon income. An example is the *alcabalá*, a
tax of 10 per cent upon every sale, which increased the
price of a commodity by that amount every time it
changed hands. This tax first restricted the sale of
goods to the vicinity of their manufacture and then
virtually destroyed Spanish industry since local tolls in
each town through which the goods passed combined
with the *alcabalá* to end production. As the yield decreased Philip raised the tax rate to 14 per cent and
tried to fix local quotas to keep up trade and bring in
revenue. The King tried to protect native industries
by prohibiting the importation of merchandise from
abroad. Smuggling of these articles followed, and the
treasury lost still more. Philip, like his father, was always pressed for funds. He tried to remedy the
steady decrease of his income by imposing new taxes
on colonial trade, on articles of food (the excise known
as the "millions"), by selling offices and indulgences,
by securing new grants from the Cortes which however
cost more to collect than they brought in, and even, in
1596, by repudiating his debts. All expedients failed
to raise the funds the King required, and worst of all,
the uneconomic nature of the imposts killed the coun-

try's productive industries and hampered her commerce. Although Spaniards did their best to carry the burden in their willing support of their monarch's defence of the faith, they could not avoid the exhaustion of their material resources and the economic depletion of their nation. With her manpower drawn away in continental wars and in colonial enterprise, by the end of Philip's reign Spain was reduced to a shell, but so courageously did she continue the national effort that the world did not realize her hollowness and still feared her as the wealthiest and most powerful of states.

ANNEXATION OF PORTUGAL

In 1580 Philip won a great political success. The dying out of the direct line of the House of Avis in Portugal left Philip as the strongest of a number of claimants for the throne. By astute diplomatic intrigue the Prudent King prepared the way and built up a considerable party among the Portuguese nobility. Of the other claimants, Don Antonio, the Prior of Crato, was the champion of the people and the representative of Portuguese nationalism. In this instance Philip proceeded with promptitude, recalled from retirement the ablest Spanish military leader, the Duke of Alva, and defeated the nationalist resistance in order to annex the adjoining kingdom. The importance of this victory was great. Not only did it achieve the age-long aim of Castile to recover the western realm but it completed the entire unification of Iberia. Still more significant was the colonial acquisition, for the annexation of Portugal brought into Philip's empire the overseas possessions of Brazil, the trading ports along the coasts of Africa, the concessions and settle-

ments in India, in Ceylon, and in the Far East, and the
ownership of the East Indies and the valuable Spice
Islands.

The domains of Portugal, added to the Spanish colonial holdings, gave Philip an empire possibly
greater in amount of territory than any one ruler
ever held. The consequences imperially were grave,
especially for the Portuguese. Thanks to the annexation, the former colonies of Portugal were now
Spanish and a prey to the attacks of Spain's enemies,
so that in the years following, England and the Dutch
attacked the eastern colonial regions. The foundation
of Holland's colonial empire in the East Indies was
the spoil, originally Portuguese-owned, captured from
Spain by the rebellious Dutch subjects of the Hapsburg. The union of the Iberian realms was to prove
impermanent; nationalism had completed the work of
the ingrained Iberian separatism and, sixty years after
Philip's annexation, Portugal broke away from the later
successor of Philip. But during the life of the Prudent
King, he gained in prestige, and his merchants profited
by the annexation since the lucrative Portuguese spice
trade was diverted through Manila and into the hands
of Spanish trading houses.

HERETIC AND MORISCO

Before turning to the colonial and maritime phases
of the history of this reign there are internal religious
factors to consider. When, in 1559, Philip returned to
the peninsula from Flanders never to leave again, one
of the chief ceremonies in his welcome was a great
auto-da-fé held at Valladolid on October 18th, one of
the most celebrated in the annals of the Spanish Inqui-

sition. While Philip had been away from Spain it was reported to him that many of the Spanish ecclesiastics were corrupt and that although the old devoted observance of religious forms prevailed, it had become mere lip-service and was hiding cynicism. The King ordered the Inquisition to redouble its efforts to hunt out looseness in church observance and to extirpate all traces of heresy. This has given rise to exaggerated accounts of the spread of Protestantism in Spain. The Inquisition was languishing for lack of material and in ferreting out small conventicles at Seville and Valladolid it magnified the danger of these few heretics, while Protestant champions have probably exaggerated the matter for propaganda. The persecutions did not involve over 200 suspects and although few of them were of the stuff of martyrs, the furor served to keep the Holy Office active until the larger Morisco inquiries.

The edicts of 1502 and of 1525-26 meant that in theory there were no longer any professing Moslems in either western or eastern realms. Any Moors still in Spain must be Christian. But everyone knew that the Moors kept many of their old ways such as the use of Arabic language and names for their children, the practice of baths and other Moslem ceremonies. Angered at this situation Philip, in 1565, set up an investigating committee and the next year despatched an Inquisition official to Granada to reform the religious practice of the Moriscos (converted Moors). From this mission, which was unnecessarily high-handed and tactless, the Moriscos became convinced that their case was desperate and when their appeals to the King brought no relief, they prepared for armed resistance. In 1568 the Morisco Wars began and for three years and a half devastated the old kingdom of Granada so that the region was ruined for some years to come. The fighting was bitter and surpassed in ferocity any of the wars of the medieval Reconquest. In these wars Don John of Austria, the illegitimate son of Charles V, born years after the death of his Empress, gained his first experience of warfare, when Philip placed him at the head of the royal forces during the course of the struggle. Upon the defeat of the Moriscos, the King deported them wholesale from their Andalusian homes to Castilian towns where they were forced to live in designated quarters under the strictest kind of surveillance. Herding these people together in city ghettos destroyed the agricultural contribution many of them had made to the prosperity of the kingdom. The sequel to this harrying of the Moors was to come in the reign of Philip's son who wrote the final chapter to the story, begun with Tarik's invasion in 711, by expelling all Moriscos from Spanish lands. Throughout Philip's persecution of the Moriscos, one may discern not only the strong religious note but also the motive of complete unification of faith and of race within the peninsula. Henceforth Spaniards could proudly boast that every tongue in their land repeated the same creed and that their king, alone of the monarchs of Christendom, tolerated no deviation from the true Church. So ardently zealous was Philip for the old ideal of religious uniformity that he was incapable of appreciating the loss to the agricultural and industrial well-being of his realms caused by the slaughter and the displacement of so many Moriscos. The final result of this intolerant policy, which the Catholic Kings had initiated and which Charles V had continued, was the serious weakening of the Spanish kingdoms by depriving them of so economically valuable and so industrious a class of the

population. Some observers see in this factor the chief
cause of the decline of the Empire, and although that
may be over-emphasis, the importance of this factor
cannot be denied.

THE INDIES—COLONIAL AND COMMERCIAL SYSTEM

Across the seas that vaster portion of the Spanish
Empire in the New World underwent important development in the years Philip II reigned and became a
great factor in making a new order in a widely expanded European civilization and political system.
The last decade of the preceding reign had been a transition period in the Spanish colonies from violence and
conquest to settled civil administration; to secure the
wealth which was the common aim of all exploring and
colonizing ventures it had become necessary to establish permanent organization for working mineral and
agricultural resources, once the initial days of gathering the "Indians' superfluous ornaments" were over.
About the year 1545 the conquerors discovered rich
deposits of silver at Zacatecas, north of Mexico City,
and at Potosí in Peru. The Zacatecas mines exceeded
the spoil of the Aztecs in value, while Potosí was even
richer than the veins of Zacatecas. To exploit these
lucrative mines the Spaniards, whose conquests had
placed them in the position of the native chieftains as
masters of the native working-class, utilized the forced
labor of the Indians. Although every ruler from the
Catholic Kings to Philip II was genuinely concerned
that the natives should be humanely treated and de-
creed that they should be Christianized, educated, and
protected, the pressure of economic interest of the colo-

nists caused many abuses of the theory of the *encomi-enda*.[1]

From the Indies was coming a steady stream of bullion and valuable natural products at the time of Philip's accession, and the form of colonial administration which had grown up under the Empire was the admiration of the rest of Europe. Evolving gradually and on a basis of maintaining the absolutism of the crown and the crown's monopoly of colonial activity, the system Philip inherited included a powerful council, the Council of the Indies, for handling political affairs and a supreme board of control for all economic matters, the *Casa de Contratación*. These bodies were the directing institutions for colonial administration at home and were completely subordinate to the king, executing his wishes but possessing no power independently of the monarch. To reflect the authority of the royal government in the New World, once the simpler early days with their governors and military commanders had given place to the more complicated situation after the conquests, the civil framework had at the top *Audiencias* and Viceroys. The *Audiencia* was originally a court but in the reign of Charles V it took on many non-judicial functions in addition to its powers as a sort of supreme court. The Viceroy came into the colonies on the heels of Cortés's victory to be the personal representative of the King of Castile and to exert

[1] About 1500, there had begun in the New World the practice of granting to Spanish proprietors parcels of land together with the forced labor of the natives living on each parcel. Such a grant, including both the land and the compulsory labor of the Indians, was known as an *encomienda*. The Spanish proprietor was ordered to instruct the natives in the Christian faith, to pay them a fair wage for their labor, and to look after their welfare. The Spanish crown endeavored thus to protect the Indians and to prevent their being enslaved.

widespread powers at the head of one of the two vast divisions of New Spain (roughly North America) and New Castile (South America). Castilian constitutional practice furnished the subdivision of the *corregimiento* into which the area of an *Audiencia* was divided, and the old democratic habit of the medieval cities came to the surface in the organization of self-governing municipalities, called *cabildos* in the Indies, wherever Spaniards made a settlement. The Hapsburg kings and their colonial officials had scant fondness for autonomous or democratic governments, the elected officers of the *cabildo* gave way to crown appointees, and the position of the *cabildo* declined though the tradition remained. The whole system was closely knit and, as far as the obstacles of distance and slow communication permitted, arranged to give effect in the colonies to the king's will.

Exclusiveness and monopoly were the keynotes of Spain's colonial policy, a policy thoroughly mercantilist in nature. That is, the colonies were to produce mineral wealth and raw materials for the benefit of the mother country and were to constitute a market for goods from home. The Spaniards in America were not allowed to produce things which would compete with Spanish products; the settlers were strictly forbidden to trade with any nation but Spain. The Catholic Kings established Cadiz as the sole port of departure and entry, to and from the New World. In 1503 Seville replaced Cadiz as the specified port and remained through the 16th century the center for all trade with the Indies. This limitation of maritime activity to the single port made it possible to exercise rigid oversight and to hold the crown's monopoly of the economic advantages derived from the colonies. Land grants and trading privileges were in the gift of the monarch, to whom came dues and shares of the yield from American sources. The *quinto*, or royal fifth of the treasure found or mined in the New World, is an example of the profit of the monopoly to the ruler. Exclusivism reached to the personnel of the colonists going out; to avoid contaminating the converted Indians with disbelief or heresy the *Casa de Contratación* had the duty of scrutinising all emigrants to make sure that they were Castilians with at least four generations of Christian blood behind them.

To maintain the close Spanish monopoly and to guard the returning wealth of the Indies from piratical attack, Philip, in 1561, instituted the system of convoyed fleets for American shipments. Great fleets of armed merchantmen, protected by fighting galleons, sailed from Seville twice a year. One, known as the *flota*, sailed in the summer and, after touching at Havana, made the port of Vera Cruz to take care of the trade of the viceroyalty of New Spain. The other, called the *galeones*, set out from Spain between January and March, touched at Cartagena on the Caribbean shore of South America, and reached the chief port of the voyage at Porto Bello on the isthmus of Panama. At Cartagena, Porto Bello, and Jalapa (a town in Mexico inland from Vera Cruz) the arrival of *galeones* and *flota* was the signal for the holding of large fairs which were the chief means of exchange and distribution of gold and goods between mother country and colonies. The two convoys joined at Havana and returned together, bringing bullion and valuable products home. Fair and fleet alike worked to keep the trade closely under regulation; the limitation of participating merchants to a few carefully controlled houses, organized into trade gilds (*consulados*), further aided the monopolistic restriction of colonial commerce. The cupidity of other nations was aroused at the actual and reported richness of the Spanish-American trade and, since outsiders were forbidden any part in this rich field, it is not surprising that energetic and adventurous men should have sought to break into the monopoly by force. In addition to the temptation to seize some of this display of wealth, Englishmen were on the threshold of a maritime revival and at times French, Dutch, and English seamen had the incentive of national enmity to urge them on to attack the Spanish Empire through its commerce and colonies.

THE INDIES—EXTENSION OF SPANISH POSSESSIONS

Before turning to the great topic of the sea operations of Philip's Empire, however, it is necessary to indicate something of the expansion of settlement in the Indies during the reign. In both the northern and southern hemispheres further exploration increased geographical knowledge and paved the way for advancing colonial development. In New Spain such discoveries as the Zacatecas deposits started mining rushes and carried settlers into the regions north of Mexico City, opening new provinces from the Gulf of California across to the Gulf of Mexico. To the southward in the other viceroyalty of New Castile, the wave of settlement pushed into the Andes from the old centers in Peru and drove fortified posts farther into the country of the warlike Araucanian Indians in Chile. The greatest advance in this viceroyalty was east of the mountains in modern Argentina and Paraguay. Under the able leadership of a Captain-general, Juan

de Garay, acting for the absent governor of the Plata
province, settlement moved out into the country between the river and the mountains; Garay made the
permanent establishment of Buenos Aires in 1580 and
developed the germs of the grazing industry, destined
to produce more wealth than the mines of the continent.
In the Philippines as well, this period witnessed significant accomplishment. After the expedition of Villalobos, Spanish activity in the Far East languished
until in 1564 the Viceroy of New Spain sent out four
ships from the Mexican port of Navidad to renew the
earlier occupation of the Philippines. Under the command of Miguel Lopez de Legaspi this venture proved
highly successful and permanently added the archipelago to the Empire of Philip II as a settled and productive colony. Legaspi accomplished great things;
he discovered the Marshall Islands on the way westward, he captured a number of the islands of the Philippine group and brought their native chiefs into a sort
of semi-feudal obedience to himself as representative
of his king, he founded the city of Manila in 1571,
which he made the capital, and, with the assistance of
the friars he carried with him, he facilitated the work
of settlement by gaining ascendancy over the natives.
As a result of saving a Chinese junk from shipwreck,
Legaspi secured friendly contact with the Celestial
Empire which brought valuable trading relations to
him and his successors. After 1580 Philip diverted
much of the old Portuguese spice trade through Manila
and the shipments of spices, silks, gems, and other oriental commodities went from the Philippines to Mexico to be trans-shipped on the convoyed plate fleets
from Vera Cruz to Spain. The monopoly system ruled
in this commerce; goods from the Orient could be car-

ried only on a convoy, known as the *Manila Galleon*, and the goods were strictly limited in kind and amount, as in the case of the trade to the Indies. One of Legaspi's lieutenants had discovered the Great Circle route in returning from the Philippines, with the consequence that all Spanish ships sailed eastward until they struck the coast of California and then turned southward to one of the Pacific ports of Mexico. An interesting outgrowth of this Philippine commerce was a stimulus to Spanish occupation of territory in California. Partly because of the length of the voyage from Manila (ninety days in the most favorable weather) and the sufferings of the crews from scurvy, and partly because of attacks on this rich shipping by English freebooters, it was desirable to have fortified posts on the California coasts to let the crews break the journey, obtain fresh water and food, and secure refuge against hostile forces at sea. This hastened materially the establishment of settlement in California during Philip's reign.

MARITIME STRENGTH AND RELATIONS WITH ENGLAND

This powerful, thriving, expanding Spanish Empire —and one must remember that the first three decades of Philip's reign had brought no serious reverse—received its greatest setback from England and by the agency of sea-power. The strength Spain had possessed on the Mediterranean throughout the century was increased during Philip's reign and that naval prestige extended outside the Straits of Gibraltar to the open ocean, where the imperial needs of Spain had produced fleets of sailing ships. These ships, of which the most celebrated were of the type called galleons,

were larger than the carracks of the Portuguese and had evolved from the oar-propelled galleys through the intermediate type known as the galleass, from which their name had come.

The galley power however meant nothing material beyond the Mediterranean for the tempestuous Atlantic was too much for the shallow, low-freeboard, rowed craft from the tideless, land-locked sea. Yet after two generations of exploring and colonizing experience Philip's Empire had built up sailing strength and Spain could boast an imposing oceanic tonnage. Of the national rivals, France had shown maritime activity both in the Mediterranean and on the ocean, and England had made enormous progress under Henry VIII with stimulus from the king's interest in a navy and from the private initiative of the rising merchant adventurers.[1]

[1] Henry is credited with personally inventing a new type of ship and with having so sound an understanding of gunnery principles that he advocated firing broadsides from sailing vessels as a major element in tactics. He was the friend and patron of the shipwright Fletcher of Rye, who in 1539, using a fore-and-aft rig, demonstrated successfully the revolutionary feat of tacking against the wind; this was the first time man had ever sailed into the wind and it may be taken as the first sign of the modern sailing age. In 1546, the year before he died, Henry issued the act establishing "The Office of the Admiralty and Marine Affairs," the foundation of the modern Admiralty. During England's participation in the Hapsburg-Valois wars the merchants profitably combined patriotism and business by fitting out privateers to prey on enemy commerce in the narrow seas, notably between 1545 and 1547. Just after Henry VIII died, a group of merchant-adventurers commissioned Sir Hugh Willoughby to search for the northeast passage around Scandinavia to the Orient. This expedition lost its leader en route but the second in command, Chancellor, pushed on into the White Sea, journeyed overland to Moscow and returned to London in 1554. An outgrowth of this venture was the formation by the merchants of the Muscovy Company, the charter for which curiously enough bore the signature of Philip II as consort of Queen Mary (1555).

In Philip's later years the enterprising rebels of the Low Countries made great strides in maritime development, uniting the sea-faring habits of a coastal folk with the capitalistic vision of an old mercantile tradition.

From the standpoint of his continental interests Philip's relations with England were vital all through his reign. His marriage to Mary Tudor had failed to yield the expected political advantage and when, upon Mary's death in 1558, her half-sister Elizabeth succeeded to the throne, Philip tried to perpetuate the English alliance by proposing himself as a suitor for the young queen's hand. She refused the offer and, since the circumstances of her birth practically compelled her to be a Protestant, there were religious as well as personal reasons for hostility between the two countries. In addition, a strong political cause for enmity lay in the rebellion of the Low Countries. Appreciating the danger of Philip's using the Netherlands as a base for any operations against England, Elizabeth winked at the seizure by her subjects of treasure and supply ships destined for the Duke of Alva in Flanders, urged other rulers to help the Dutch keep on with their revolt, and adroitly led her Valois suitors to aid William of Orange. All this Elizabeth did while officially and ostensibly at peace with Philip, for she had sound reasons for fearing war until she had strengthened her precarious hold on the English crown and she wisely saw that only by letting the foreign situation develop without seeming to force it, could she rally all shades of opinion in England to her support.

On his side too, Philip was reluctant to engage in war with England. In the early years, thanks to

Elizabeth's diplomacy, he had hopes of regaining the old alliance; he always had a host of other problems on his hands and he had a strong legalistic reason for keeping peace with the heretic queen. Legally the Catholic Mary Queen of Scots (Mary Stuart) had a strong claim to the English throne, but she was a niece of the Duke of Guise and the widow of the short-lived Valois, Francis II, who had reigned in France from 1559 to 1560. Both of the French families with whom Mary was connected, Philip disliked and suspected; he had no intention of adding to their influence and consequently he would not try to drive Elizabeth from her throne to aggrandize a member of the Guise house. On the other hand he respected Mary's right at law and he waited until a victory over Elizabeth would leave him free to take the English crown himself. This element in the political situation helped restrain Philip from war during years of English depredations on his ships and on the coasts of his Empire. Finally, in 1587, Elizabeth reluctantly executed Mary Stuart, who had been driven out of her kingdom of Scotland to take refuge in England some years before, and who had served as a center of plots against Elizabeth. Then at last the way was clear for Philip to move against the heretical and piratical English and to defend both the faith and Spain's Empire by crushing the rising power of England on the water. Moreover, in 1585 Elizabeth, conscious that the murder of William of Orange the year before and the failure of France to support the Dutch were diminishing the resistance to Spain, had at last come further into the open and had agreed to send 6,000 men under the Earl of Leicester to aid the rebellion in Holland. Yet, although Elizabeth had given sure evidence of unfriendly conduct toward

Spain and although Philip had for years encouraged
Catholic plots in England, the practice of the period
permitted both monarchs to remain formally at peace
with each other.

Alongside the grievances occasioned by the European situation, the rivalry between England and the
Spanish Empire had brought conflict and injury on the
sea and in Philip's colonies. As indicated above,
both France and England resented their exclusion
from the rich colonial field Spain had monopolized in
the New World and found it hard to resist the temptation to seize Spanish ships and plunder the wealth
of the Indies. A color of legality came from letters of
marque issued by such enemies of Spain as France,
during time of war, and the rebellious Low Countries.
Religion played a part too, for Huguenots, Dutch, and
Englishmen could assert that their Protestantism jus-
tified them in robbing the great persecutor of their
sects. Some of the privateers were undoubtedly sin-
cere in their religious incentive, but many were far
more concerned with the acquisition of booty than
with vengeance for the severities of the Inquisition.
Also the line between a privateer's semi-legal attack on
a foe and a pirate's lawless plundering was slender and
not easy to fix in the 16th century. For example, the
Beggars of the Sea, the naval contingents from the
Low Country ports who were effective in harassing
the Spanish forces, were so greedy for spoil that they
became the terror of friend and foe alike.

HUGUENOT INCURSIONS

From France, and especially from French Huguenots, Philip had experienced acts of maritime aggres-

sion. Piratical attacks were not uncommon; in 1555 the French corsair Jacques de Sorie sacked and burned Havana. Some years later a Norman sea-captain, Jean Ribaut, made a tentative effort to plant a post on the east coast of the present state of Florida. Although this effort failed, it had enjoyed the patronage of Admiral Coligny (the great leader of the Huguenots), and the approval of the Queen-mother. The Admiral sent out another expedition under Laudonnière in 1564. This time the French established Fort Caroline at the mouth of the Saint John's River, a settlement which particularly alarmed the Spanish authorities because it lay on the course of the treasure fleets and commanded the approach to Havana. The fact that the interlopers were heretics added hatred to the Spaniards' sense of strategic menace. As soon as word of Laudonnière's foundation reached Philip, he ordered Pedro Menendez de Áviles, the commander of the last fleet to New Spain, to drive out the French. Menendez led a large force from Cadiz, landed in Florida in September, 1565, and began the foundation of Saint Augustine. With stern energy Menendez devoted himself to crushing the enemies of his king and his faith and practically exterminated the entire French party. Catherine de' Medici and Frenchmen of both religions demanded reparation for what they considered a massacre but Philip refused to make amends and replied that the French had no right to invade Spanish territory. The Valois were unable to break with Philip at the time, but a private adventurer, Dominique de Gourgues, avenged his countrymen by killing the garrison of Spaniards at the former Fort Caroline and plundering three treasure ships on the way home. A

somewhat similar attempt to establish a colony for
Huguenots in South America had led in 1555 to the
building of Fort Coligny on a rocky island in the Bay
of Rio de Janeiro in Brazil. The leader of the colony,
the arbitrary and erratic explorer Villegagnon, was unable to repel the attack of the Portuguese governor and
the Huguenots were driven off while the governor established the Portuguese town of Rio de Janeiro to
prevent the return of the French. Nearer home Philip
fought two naval engagements with the French. After
the annexation of Portugal, the pretender Antonio of
Crato secured from Catherine de' Medici a great fleet
of fifty-five ships under the celebrated French mer-
cenary admiral, Leon Strozzi. In the summer of 1582
Don Antonio sailed to Terceira in the Azores only to
meet utter defeat at the hands of Philip's able captain,
the Marquis of Santa Cruz, who destroyed the fleet
and killed Strozzi in the battle. Don Antonio escaped
and a year later suffered the same fate in the same
waters, when Santa Cruz smashed the Portuguese pretender's hired French squadron with its company of
6,000 men. These actions in the Azores raised still
higher the prestige of Philip's navy, reinforcing the
reputation won by Lepanto.

RISE OF ENGLISH FREEBOOTERS

But though the Prudent King might defeat French
captains and fleets, the mariners of England had gained
confidence in their ability to defy the naval might of
the Spanish Empire. Impelled by the desire for trade,
English merchants had been sending out ships to break
into the forbidden zones of the Spanish and Portuguese

Empires.[1] For these ventures several merchants joined
together, frequently including as shareholders high officials of the state and even the Queen herself, supplied
ships, met all necessary expenses, and then divided the
profits of the voyage according to the share each participating "Adventurer" had put into the speculation.
This arrangement was highly satisfactory to Elizabeth
for several reasons. On the one hand she reaped large
profit from many of the cruises; from Drake's voyage
around the world she received a private share of the
spoil amounting to a present value of $450,000 on her
investment of $1,250. Then too, the English captains
struck heavy blows at the colonial strength of her
enemy Philip, which she could stoutly claim were private acts of individuals when Philip protested or demanded reparation, and these privately built ships
saved her the expense of a big navy and accomplished
much the same end.

A pioneer in invading the Spanish monopoly was
the Devonshire gentleman John Hawkins, son of
old William Hawkins of Plymouth who had made
a voyage to Guinea and Brazil in Henry VIII's
time. Having made several trading trips to the Canary
Islands, John Hawkins had learned from friends in
those islands that negro slaves were in great demand in
the Spanish Indies. Las Casas and other champions of
the Indians had advocated relieving the American na-

[1] The great authority on this subject, Sir Julian Corbett (in
Drake and the Tudor Navy, Vol. I, 74-76), states that the causes
of the Anglo-Spanish conflict were threefold. To the people it was
mainly religious in nature, to the government it was political—the
defence of the new British nationality against a dominant Spanish
Empire—and to the merchants it was commercial. The aggressive
tactics of the merchants provided trained men and the money to
fight Philip and the pushing of the heretics' trade into his domains
gave Philip no alternative but war.

tives by importing Africans to work the plantations in the New World, but the royal monopoly was understocking the market and keeping the price of slaves high. In 1562 Hawkins sailed on his first slaving trip; with slaves secured from West Africa against the will of the Portuguese proprietors of Guinea, he found ready sale to the Spanish planters of Española and New Spain, and made a gain of 60 per cent on the venture. A second voyage to the Spanish Main followed, but on Hawkins' third attempt he forced his way into several harbors of the Indies and finally was severely handled at San Juan de Ulloa, near Vera Cruz. The return of the survivors of this action brought a tale of Spanish treachery and barbarous treatment of the English captives which fired England with wrath and inspired a host of sea-captains with hatred of Spain.

DRAKE

With Hawkins at San Juan de Ulloa was his kinsman Francis Drake, also well-born and also a native of Devon. The exploits of Hawkins had created a great stir in England and brought adventurous emulators; his energetic commerce had made him wealthy and his nautical skill and patriotism brought him knighthood and high rank in the Queen's service. Drake was of the same stuff but he surpassed Hawkins in maritime genius and in renown. The year 1570 marked a general change in the tactics of Drake and Hawkins and of the many English captains who had been following the lead of these two celebrated Devonmen, a change from trading incursions to such acts of piracy as robbing the treasure ships en route to Seville and plundering New World ports. In 1572 Drake boldly accomplished the almost incredible feat of invading the strong port of Nombre de Dios on the Caribbean side of Darien and capturing the mule-train which was bringing the annual consignment of treasure from the mines of Peru. In 1578 he set out aboard the *Golden Hind* for the South Sea, defeated and plundered many Spanish galleons, raided points in Philip's Empire in all the oceans and from the Straits of Magellan up the Pacific coast of New Castile and New Spain to Drake's Bay in California. Off that shore he attacked the *Manila Galleon* and proceeded across the Pacific; after touching at several of the Moluccas, Drake completed the second circumnavigation of the globe by reaching England in September, 1580. In spite of the Spanish ambassador's vigorous demands that Drake be punished as a pirate, Elizabeth made a visit of state to the port of Deptford and knighted the great captain on the deck of the *Golden Hind*. Drake's exploit was monumental in every way; he had successfully defied the might of a powerful empire, he had gained enormous treasure, he had frightened Spaniards on the Pacific into believing that he had found the Strait of Anian or the Northwest Passage, and he had gained the open recognition of his sovereign. It is small wonder that for generations Spanish-American mothers quieted their children by saying, "Drake is coming." It is to be borne in mind that Drake was not the only Englishman to inflict such loss upon the Spanish Empire; other freebooters of his stamp, patriots and gentlemen for the most part, were achieving similar triumphs at Philip's expense. Such were Sir Humphrey Gilbert, Martin Frobisher, Raleigh, and Davis, to name the more notable.

Philip had suffered grievous injury without receiving

any satisfaction from his complaints to the English Queen. The final blow, a severe strain to the patience of even the Prudent King, came in a joint-stock raiding venture of thirty ships which Sir Francis conducted to the Spanish Main and the West Indies in 1585-86. Although the booty was smaller than that yielded by other voyages, the raid was sufficient to bring Philip to the conviction that nothing but war could end the intolerable depredations on his Empire and settle the issue of supremacy between himself and the heretic queen with her pirate brood.

WAR WITH ENGLAND

The war, which Elizabeth unlike her subjects accepted reluctantly, was to be memorable for the defeat of Philip's great fleet, the famous Spanish Armada, the name of which, *Armada Invencible* or "Invincible Fleet," reflected Spain's hopes of success. By the spring of 1587 it was known that the King of Spain was preparing his ships to attack England and Drake with difficulty gained the Queen's consent to "impeach the joining together of the King of Spain's fleet." Sir Francis courageously entered Cadiz harbor and burned, sank, and captured over thirty craft concentrating there. Then he took possession of Cape Saint Vincent to cut the line of approach to Santa Cruz's main base at Lisbon, an interesting anticipation of later sound naval strategy. Lack of support and of supplies forced Drake to return to England, having prevented the sailing of the Armada that year. Philip persisted in his plans, however, undaunted even by the death in January, 1588, of his experienced admiral Santa Cruz, and the fleet left Lisbon on May 20th. In his meticulous

way the King drew up a detailed plan for his fleet. It
was to sail up the Channel, drive off the enemy squadron covering the Flemish coast, and convoy the army
of the Duke of Parma, which was to be in readiness on
the shore, across to the conquest of England. Elizabeth's weak army was no match for Parma's veteran
tercios of the splendid Spanish infantry. The account
of the defeat of the Invincible Armada at the hands of
the swift-sailing, hard-hitting English fleet two months
later, is too well known to need repetition here. In
that action it is to be observed that there was a conflict between opposing naval theories, significant for
the future. The Spanish style of large ship, with its
towering structures forward and aft and its few, rather
weak guns, was designed for close fighting by running
alongside an enemy, boarding and using its force of
soldiers in an infantry combat on the decks. The English great-ship was "race-built," that is, she had flush
decks and was less cumbersome and more easily handled in the wind; the ordnance was heavier, of longer
range, and more numerous than aboard the Spanish
galleons, enabling gunnery to decide battles. Hence in
the running combats up the Channel, the more un-
wieldy and weaker-gunned Spaniards were at the mercy
of the English with their better seamanship and greater
weight of metal.

The war continued through the remaining ten
years of Philip's life, chiefly naval in character.
Although Philip seized bases on the coast of Brit-
tany to send armies into Ireland or England, the
decisive feature of sea-power asserted itself, for the
veteran Spanish troops could do no harm to England
as long as Elizabeth's ships controlled the seas. The
English privateers and some of the Queen's ships con-

tinued to take toll of Spanish merchantmen so that the
war was profitable to England and costly to imperial
Spain. Yet the only later English victory was the capture of Cadiz in 1596 and that was bungled enough to
let the Spanish destroy their galleons and keep the
riches out of the victors' hands. In 1589 Drake headed
an expeditionary force to Portugal which ended in dis-
aster and in 1595 both he and Sir John Hawkins died
in the course of an unsuccessful joint attack on the
Indies. The fiasco in 1589 and a lull of two years gave
Philip time to rebuild his shattered fleet; in 1591 his
force was strong enough to drive off Lord Thomas
Howard from an attempt to intercept the *flota* in the
Azores. It was in this action that Sir Richard Gren-
ville, who had disobeyed Howard's order to retire, lost
the *Revenge* in a hopeless, single-handed fight. The
next year Howard again failed to injure the *flota* off
the Azores, although he did seize a Portuguese spice
ship sailing alone.

DEATH OF PHILIP—SEA-POWER TRIUMPHANT

On all sides things were going badly for Philip. His
wars in France and the Low Countries as well as on
the sea were swinging against him and the financial
drain had brought impoverishment to his kingdoms and
had forced him to mortgage the ordinary revenue and
the expected treasure from the Indies for three years
in advance. Worn out by thirty-five years of unre-
mitting toil, suffering physical anguish, but patient and
uncomplaining in the face of accumulating disasters,
confident that he had fought the good fight and had
labored well in God's cause, Philip II passed to his reward in September, 1598. Hardly suspected at the

time, the Spanish Empire was actually near the brink of material ruin as a result of his policy. The world was still dazzled by the glory and the fabulous vastness of the Empire and could not see that the seeds of its decay were already sprouting within the glittering structure. What contemporaries could appreciate, however, was that the naval war had destroyed the overwhelming preponderance of Iberia on the water. Spanish ships still sailed the oceans but they were never again to dominate the sea as they had or to guarantee the unquestioned monopoly of the Spanish colonial system. England, during the years Philip had ruled, had won a position of naval might which advanced her commerce and placed her on the way to colonial expansion. The launching of the modern era in sea-power was further shown by the beginnings, at the end of Philip's reign, of the maritime career of the Dutch, who were to contest the newly won strength of England. Technically the period had seen important developments of sailing craft and of naval tactics, a few of which have been indicated, and these developments were to bring naval science definitely out of the middle ages and into ways which have not entirely disappeared today. Finally, in the picture of Alexander of Parma, helpless on the Flemish shore with an army of incomparable Spanish infantry which was far superior to Elizabeth's land forces, we have a shining example of the rôle sea-power was to play in the coming age.

In concluding this survey it is well to remark how marvellously rapid the rise of the Spanish Empire had been and how significant for the future the history of the Empire and the attacks upon it were to prove to be. In an incredibly short time the small, disunited kingdoms of Iberia had produced the fabulous oversea possessions of Portugal and Castile. Under Charles V the Spains had become the center of preponderant world-power, acquired more suddenly than their resources could well warrant. In the reign of Philip II that Empire, increased by the annexation of Portugal, stood as the embodiment of the old ways and the old forces of European civilization. Religious uniformity, political absolutism, aristocratic domination of society, economic monopoly, in short the old privileges and the old traditionalism of medieval Europe, found their vigorous champion in the Prudent King. He staked the existence and the full strength of the Spanish Empire in the struggle to maintain those elements against the rising forces of individualism, the tide of the new age. The expansion of Europe into new worlds had created new conditions and had provided the opportunity for new commercial classes and interests, whose advance not even Philip could stay or retard.

In that conflict, maritime factors had played a leading part; the nature of sea-power changed from the age-old domination of the galley to the new capabilities of the sailing-ship, and maritime strength proved the weapon to defeat Philip's Empire. To maintain her supremacy Spain had to control the water and that control became the prize of English and Dutch traders and sea-captains. Lord Francis Bacon stated this decisive rôle of sea-power in his *Considerations touching upon a War with Spain,* by saying: "For money, no doubt it is the principal part of the greatness of Spain; for by that they maintain their veteran army; and Spain is the only State of Europe that is a money-grower. . . . Their greatness consisteth in their treasure, their treasure is in the Indies, and their Indies (if it be well weighed) are indeed but an accession to such as are masters by sea. So as this axle-tree, whereupon their greatness turneth, is soon cut in two by any that shall be stronger than they by sea."

BIBLIOGRAPHY

IT is a pleasure to acknowledge at this point my gratitude to those who have given me aid and encouragement in this undertaking. I am under special obligation to my colleague and friend, Professor Laurence B. Packard, for helpful criticism at all stages, to his co-editor, Professor Sidney R. Packard of Smith College, and to my wife, Irene L. Salmon, for assistance on the manuscript. To Professor Roger B. Merriman of Harvard University I would express my grateful appreciation for reading the manuscript and advising me, as well as for opening to me the field of Hispanic history.

This bibliography makes no pretence to completeness or exhaustiveness, but its purpose is to serve as a guide to the next step in further reading. In addition to bibliographies mentioned in works cited below, useful bibliographical works are: B. Sánchez Alonso, *Fuentes de la Historia Española* (Madrid, 1919); R. Foulché-Delbosc and L. Barrau-Dihigo, *Manuel de l'Hispanisant* (New York, 1920); C. K. Jones, *Hispanic-American Bibliographies* (Baltimore, 1922); Hayward Keniston, *List of Works for the Study of Hispanic-American History* (New York, 1920).

For the period of this study as a whole the most valuable work is Roger B. Merriman, *Rise of the Spanish Empire* (3 vols., New York, 1918-25, fourth volume to appear soon), valuable also for its extensive critical bibliographies. The best and most recent Spanish treatment is Antonio Ballesteros y Beretta, *Historia de España y su Influencia en la Historia Universal* (5 vols., Barcelona, 1918-26), with very copious bibliographical references. Another excellent work in Spanish is Rafael Altamira y Crevea, *Historia de España y de la Civilización Española* (4 vols., Barcelona, 1909-14), the last 92 pages of which contain a bibliographical guide.

Based on Altamira is the one volume *History of Spain* of C. E. Chapman (New York, 1925). An older book emphasizing the Spanish contribution to general civilization is *The Spanish People*, by Martin A. S. Hume (New York, 1901). A clear and compact general history is Gustav Diercks, *Geschichte Spaniens* (2 vols., Berlin, 1895-96). In spite of some carelessness in details, Salvador de Madariaga's *Spain* (London, 1930) has brilliant qualities as has his collection of literary essays, *The Genius of Spain* (Oxford, 1923). For the general European view one should consult also the appropriate chapters in E. Lavisse and A. Rambaud (editors), *Histoire Générale du IV siècle à nos jours* (12 vols., Paris, 1893-96), especially chapter 9 of volume IV and chapter 2 of volume V. Similarly the *Cambridge Medieval History* (1911- six volumes so far) and the *Cambridge Modern History* (14 vols., 1902-10) contain pertinent chapters and have, like the Lavisse and Rambaud, lengthy but uncritical bibliographies. Brief accounts may be found in textbooks of Latin American history such as, among many others, W. S. Robertson, *History of the Latin-American Nations* (New York, 1926) and the recent *People and Politics of Latin America* by Mary W. Williams (Boston, 1930).

Specialized topics up to the time of the Catholic Kings:

W. Z. Ripley, *The Races of Europe* (New York, 1899), sane and reliable on controversial ethnological questions.

Roman period—E. S. Bouchier, *Spain under the Roman Empire* (Oxford, 1914); the fifth volume of Theodor Mommsen's *Römische Geschichte*, translated by W. P. Dickson as *The Provinces of the Roman Empire* (2 vols., London, 1909).

Visigothic Spain—Sir Charles Oman, *Dark Ages* (London, 1903); *Cambridge Medieval History* (1913), chapter 6 of volume II, by Rafael Altamira.

Moorish Spain—Reinhart Dozy, *Histoire des Musulmans d'Espagne* (1861), translated by F. G. Stokes as *Spanish Islam* (London, 1913), work of a great Dutch Orientalist; Al Makkarî, *The History of the Mohammedan Dynasties in Spain* (translated and edited by Pascual de Gayangos, 2 vols., London, 1840-43), by a 16th century Moor, highly useful; Ameer Ali, *Short History of the Saracens* (London, 1900), by a modern Moslem; Stanley Lane-Poole, *Moors in Spain* (London, 1887), popular and uneven; Ernest Mercier, *Histoire de l'Afrique septentrionale* (3 vols., Paris, 1888-91), standard for North Africa.

Christian kingdoms—M. Colmeiro, *Reyes Cristianos desde Alonso VI hasta Alfonso XI* (Madrid, 1901); J. Zurita, *Anales de la Corona de Aragon* (6 vols., Saragossa, 1610); *The Chronicle of James I King of Aragon*, translated by J. Forster (2 vols., London, 1883); A. Herculano, *Historia de Portugal* (4th edition, 4 vols., Lisbon, 1875-88), down to 1279; H. Morse Stephens, *Story of Portugal* (New York, 1901), in Story of the Nations Series.

Medieval Spanish institutions—M. Colmeiro, *Curso de Derecho Político* (Madrid, 1873); R. B. Merriman, article on "The Cortes of the Spanish Kingdoms in the later Middle Ages" in *American Historical Review*, vol. XVI, no. 3 (1911).

The Catholic Kings:

William H. Prescott, *History of the Reign of Ferdinand and Isabella* (3 vols., numerous editions, first in 1837), the standard work; J-H. Mariéjol, *L'Espagne sous Ferdinand et Isabelle* (Paris, 1892), good for social, economic, and intellectual phases; H. C. Lea, *A History of the Inquisition of Spain* (4 vols., New York, 1906-07), and *The Inquisition in the Spanish Dependencies* (New York, 1908), authoritative and brilliant.

For foreign affairs, the bibliographical notes in the second volume of Merriman furnish an excellent guide and supplement Prescott. See also: H. Lemonnier's volume in Lavisse's *Histoire de France* (vol. V, part 2, Paris), for French side; H. A. L. Fisher's volume (1485-1547) in the *Political History of England* (2d edition, London, 1919, chs. 2, 4, 5) and volume I of Wilhelm Busch's *England under the Tudors* (London, 1895), for English side; L.

von Ranke, *Die Osmanen und die Spanische Monarchie* (3d edition, Berlin, 1857), runs through the 16th century. Discovery and colonization:

C. Raymond Beazley, *The Dawn of Modern Geography* (3 vols., London, 1897-1906), and his *Prince Henry the Navigator* (New York, 1895), best life of the Navigator, containing a compact summary of geographical ideas of middle ages; J. P. Oliveira Martins, *The Golden Age of Prince Henry the Navigator* (trans., London, 1914), standard Portuguese work; J. A. Williamson, *Maritime Enterprise, 1485-1558* (Oxford, 1913), the voyages and motives behind them; C. de Lannoy and H. vander Linden, *Histoire de l'expansion coloniale des peuples européens: Portugal et Espagne* (Paris, 1907), general account; the first volume of Edward Channing's *A History of the United States* (New York, 1905), and the first volume of Justin Winsor's (ed.) *Narrative and Critical History of America* (Boston, 1884), are useful; Henry Vignaud, *Histoire critique de la grande entreprise de Christophe Colomb* (2 vols., Paris, 1911), best work among vast amount of material on Columbus.

E. G. Bourne, *Spain in America* (New York, 1904), extremely valuable, covers all Spanish colonization in North America, gives sound criticism of the authorities; E. P. Cheyney, *European Backgrounds of American History* (New York, 1904), chapters 1-5 and 9-10 are illuminating for this period; Clarence H. Haring, *Trade and Navigation between Spain and the Indies in the time of the Hapsburgs* (Cambridge, Mass., 1918), indispensable work on economic and maritime side of Spanish colonial system, with valuable bibliographical information also; E. J. Hamilton's article, "Wages and Subsistence on Spanish Treasure Ships, 1503-1660" in *Journal of Political Economy* (XXXVII, no. 5, 1929), concrete and revealing.

K. G. Jayne, *Vasco da Gama and his Successors* (London, 1910); H. Morse Stephens, *Affonso de Albuquerque* (Oxford, 1912); F. C. Danvers, *The Portuguese in India*

(2 vols., London, 1894); the chapter in the fourth volume of Lavisse et Rambaud by M. L. Gallois, *Les Portugais: Leurs Découvertes et Colonisations en Afrique et en Asie,* all of the above are useful for the Portuguese Empire in the East. Admiral G. A. Ballard, *Rulers of the Indian Ocean* (Boston, 1928), account of Portuguese and Dutch in the East, with the advantage of the author's being familiar with the area in question, but with the defect of lacking references. Richard Hakluyt, *The Principall Navigations, Voiages and Discoveries of the English Nation* . . . (first published 1589-90, many editions since) the great epic of the English voyages; G. B. Parks, *Richard Hakluyt and the English Voyages* (New York, 1928), thorough discussion of Hakluyt, his work, and the current of the time; Walter Raleigh, *The English Voyages of the 16th Century* (Glasgow, 1928), literary emphasis predominant.

Reign of Charles V:

In addition to the third volume of Merriman, Edward Armstrong's *The Emperor Charles V* (2 vols., London, 1902) is excellent; F. López de Gomara, *Anales de Carlos Quinto* (ed. and trans. by R. B. Merriman, 1912), contemporary chronicle; H. L. Seaver, *The Great Revolt in Castile* (Boston, 1928), good presentation of internal conditions during the Comunero revolt; F. A. Mignet, *Rivalité de François I et de Charles Quint* (2 vols., Paris, 1876), minute account of relations with France to 1529; L. von Pastor, *History of the Popes* (ed. and trans. by R. F. Kerr, 18 vols., London, 1902-29), authoritative for both papal affairs and European conditions; E. Charrière, *Négociations de la France dans le Levant* (4 vols., Paris, 1848-60), in the French *Collection de Documents Inédits,* for relations of the Turks with western nations; C. Fernández Duro, *Armada Española* (9 vols., Madrid, 1895-1903), first three volumes for this study, sound for general naval history of Spain, for the wars with Turks and corsairs, and for New World voyages.

On conquests and colonial expansion of the reign, the voluminous printed works are headed by the classic accounts of Prescott, *History of the Conquest of Mexico* (3 vols., New York, 1843), and *History of the Conquest of Peru* (2 vols., New York, 1848). Other useful studies include: C. R. Markham, *The Conquest of New Granada* (New York, 1912); Bernard Moses, *The Establishment of Spanish Rule in America* (New York, 1898), and *The Spanish Dependencies in South America* (2 vols., London, 1914); the first four chapters of H. E. Bolton, *Spanish Borderlands* (New Haven, 1912), the fifth chapter treats of the Florida episodes in reign of Philip II; Woodbury Lowery, *The Spanish Settlements within the present limits of the United States, 1513-1561* (New York, 1901). Portions of contemporary accounts appear in two volumes of the *Original Narratives of Early American History*, edited by J. F. Jameson, entitled *Spanish Explorers in the Southern United States, 1528-1543* and *Spanish Exploration in the Southwest, 1542-1706*.

Reign of Philip II:

M. A. S. Hume, *Philip II of Spain* (London, 1897), brief life; H. Forneron, *Histoire de Philippe II* (2d edn., 2 vols., Paris, 1881), more detailed; W. H. Prescott, *History of the reign of Philip the Second* (3 vols., Boston, 1855-58), incomplete, covers about half the reign; Luis Cabrera de Cordoba, *Felipe Segundo, Rey de España* (4 vols., Madrid, 1876-77), contemporary account, first published in 1619; chapter 2 in volume five of Lavisse et Rambaud, *L'Œuvre de Philippe II*, by J-H. Mariéjol.

Phases of internal history—M. Philippson, *Ein Ministerium unter Philipp II* (Berlin, 1895), ministry of Cardinal Granvelle in Spain; Marquis de Pidal, *Historia de las alteraciones en Aragon* (Madrid, 1862); L. P. Gachard, *Don Carlos et Philippe II* (Brussels, 1863); F. W. C. Lieder, "The Don Carlos Theme" in *Harvard Studies in Philology and Literature* (vol. XII, Cambridge,

1930), an interesting study of the literary influence of this prince's story; H. C. Lea, *Moriscos of Spain* (Philadelphia, 1901), scholarly and clear; Diego Hurtado de Mendoza, *Guerra de Granada* (Valencia, 1795), contemporary account by a great statesman and one of the greatest Castilian grandees; J. Estébanez Calderon, *La conquista y perdida de Portugal* (Madrid, 1885), for the annexation of Portugal; in French translation, J. Conestaggio, *Histoire de la Réunion de Portugal à la couronne de Castile* (Paris, 1680).

Foreign relations—in addition to some of the books above, J. W. Thompson, *Wars of Religion in France* (Chicago, 1909), excellent for politics, 1559-76; J-H. Mariéjol, *Catherine de Médicis, 1519-89* (Paris, 1920), notable and able, also his volume in Lavisse, *Histoire de France,* for years 1559-98 (vol. 6, part 1, Paris); M. Philippson, *Westeuropa im Zeitalter von Philipp II, Elizabeth und Heinrich IV* (Berlin, 1882), for general diplomatic relations.

For the revolt of the Netherlands—J. L. Motley, *The Rise of the Dutch Republic* (3 vols., London, 1856) and *History of the United Netherlands* (4 vols., London, 1860-67), discount the intense Protestant bias; J. P. Blok, *History of the People of the Netherlands* (trans. by Ruth Putnam, 4 vols., New York, 1898-1907), volumes 2 and 3, presents the Dutch side; Cardinal Bentivoglio, *Della Guerra di Fiandra* (English trans., London, 1652); A. J. Namèche, *Guillaume le Taciturne et la révolution des Pays-Bas au XVI siècle* (Louvain, 1890); Ruth Putnam, *William the Silent, Prince of Orange* (2 vols., New York, 1895); Sir William Stirling-Maxwell, *Don John of Austria* (2 vols., London, 1883), valuable also for the Lepanto campaign and naval wars in the Mediterranean.

Other material on the maritime struggles with the Moslem may be found in Duro, cited above, in C. Manfroni, *Storia della marina italiana* (Rome, 1897), in C. de la

Roncière, *Histoire de la Marine Française* (5 vols., Paris, 1906-23), and in Stanley Lane-Poole, *The Barbary Corsairs* (New York, 1890), popular and not always accurate in details. Bibliographical help on this topic may be secured from M. F. de Navarrete, *Biblioteca Maritima Española* (2 vols., Madrid, 1851). A convenient account of the history of Moroccan piracy is to be found in Robert Brown's introduction to the Hakluyt Society's publication of *The Adventures of Thomas Pellow* (London, 1890).

For relations with England—J. A. Froude, *History of England* (12 vols., London, 1856-70), a classic, volumes 7-12 covering the reign of Elizabeth are fairer on the whole than the earlier portion, though one must be on guard against Froude's partiality and dramatic vision of history, here exaggerating the heroic qualities of Burghley and the wickedness of Mary Stuart; Mandell Creighton, *The Age of Elizabeth* (London, 1876), brilliant survey; A. F. Pollard, *History of England from the Accession of Edward VI to the Death of Elizabeth* (London, 1910); E. P. Cheyney, *A History of England from the Defeat of the Armada to the Death of Elizabeth* (2 vols., New York, 1914-26), thorough study of the end of the reign, particularly valuable for the later phases of the naval war with Spain; Conyers Read, *Mr. Secretary Walsingham and the Policy of Elizabeth* (3 vols., Cambridge, Mass., 1925), penetrating and scholarly study of Elizabethan foreign affairs; M. A. S. Hume, *Two English Queens and Philip* (London, 1898).

On the maritime and colonial rivalries the best single work is Sir Julian Corbett's *Drake and the Tudor Navy* (2 vols., London, 1898), with excellent discussion of naval elements and of the general situation, and with helpful bibliographical material. His *Successors of Drake* (London, 1900) should also be noted. Very valuable too for its breadth and scholarliness is J. A. Williamson's *Sir John Hawkins, the Time and the Man* (Oxford, 1927).

C. Fernández Duro's *Armada Española* is good for this period, and his *La Armada Invencible* (2 vols., Madrid, 1884-85) is one of the best accounts of the Armada action and prints the important Spanish sources. Another reliable treatment is W. F. Tilton, *Die Katastrophe der Spanischen Armada* (Freiburg, 1894). Hakluyt's *Principall Navigations* and the publications by the Hakluyt Society of contemporary works contain the English accounts of the maritime enterprises leading up to the naval war. See also: J. A. Froude, *English Seamen in the 16th Century* (London, 1895), sparkling but unsound and prejudiced, worth reading if not believing; his *The Spanish Story of the Armada* (London, 1892); M. A. S. Hume, *The Year after the Armada* (London, 1896); C. F. Duro, *La Conquista de las Azores en 1583* (Madrid, 1886); Sir Edwin Pears' article, "The Spanish Armada and the Ottoman Porte" in the *English Historical Review* (vol. VIII, 439-466), discussing Elizabeth's efforts to stir up the Turks against Philip.

For the extension of Spanish colonies under Philip, see (in addition to works already cited): H. E. Bolton, *Spanish Exploration in the Southwest* (1916); Francis Parkman, *Pioneers of France in the New World* (Boston, various editions); M. L. Amunátegui, *Descubrimiento y conquista de Chile* (Santiago, 1913); H. I. Priestley, *Mexican Nation* (New York, 1923), good bibliography, the first seven chapters cover this period.

Additional material on the organization of the colonial system: P. Leroy Beaulieu, *De la colonization chez les peuples modernes* (Paris, 1874); Wilhelm Roscher, *The Spanish Colonial System* (translation edited by E. G. Bourne, New York, 1904); C. A. Cunningham, *The Audiencia in the Spanish Colonies* (Berkeley, 1919); Lillian E. Fisher, *Viceregal Administration in the Spanish-American Colonies* (Berkeley, 1926); Arthur S. Aiton, *Antonio de Mendoza* (Durham, 1927), a study of the first Viceroy of New Spain; Lesley B. Simpson, *The En-*

comienda in New Spain (Berkeley, 1929), a contribution
to the social as well as the economic history of the colonial
system; Laurence B. Packard, *The Commercial Revolution* (New York, 1927), in this series, the first chapter
gives a compact summary of the commercial situation at
this time; C. H. Haring's *Trade and Navigation* . . .
(cited above) is invaluable for the economic side. The
following articles in the *Hispanic-American Historical
Review* are of value: C. H. Haring, "The Genesis of
Royal Government in the Spanish Indies" (May, 1927);
C. W. Hackett, "Delimitation of Political Jurisdictions in
Spanish North America to 1535" (Feb. 1918); C. E.
Casteñeda, "The Corregidor in Spanish Colonial Admin-
istration" (Nov. 1929); W. W. Pierson, "Some Reflec-
tions on the Cabildo as an Institution" (Nov. 1922);
W. L. Schurz, "Mexico, Peru, and the Manila Galleon"
(Nov. 1918).

Sea-power—A. T. Mahan, *The Influence of Sea Power
upon History* (Boston, 1890), an epoch-making book, a
pioneer work in focusing attention on the maritime factor, the first two chapters (the Introduction and chap. I)
contain a discussion of sea-power and its elements which
is applicable to this study; another of Admiral Mahan's
works, *Naval Strategy* (Boston, 1911), consisting of lec-
tures delivered before the U. S. Naval War College, con-
tains extensive illustration of naval principles, with ex-
amples from military history; Sir Julian Corbett, *Some
Principles of Maritime Strategy* (London, 1918), of similar value, draws comparisons with principles laid down by
such authorities as Clausewitz and Jomini for land operations; P. A. Silburn, *Evolution of Sea-Power* (London,
1912), surveys ancient and medieval factors but is in-
accurate.

INDEX

149